casual cooking

Gluten & dairy free for me

casual cooking

Gluten & dairy free for me

LOVE FOOD™

This edition published by Parragon Books Ltd in 2015
LOVE FOOD is an imprint of Parragon Books Ltd

Parragon Books Ltd
Chartist House
15–17 Trim Street
Bath BA1 1HA, UK
www.parragon.com/lovefood

ISBN 978-1-4723-8486-7
Printed in China

Cover photography by Charlie Richards
Designed by Beth Kalynka
Nutritional analysis by Judith Wills

Notes for the Reader
This book uses both metric and imperial measurements. Follow the same units of measurement throughout; do not mix metric and imperial. All spoon measurements are level: teaspoons are assumed to be 5 ml, and tablespoons are assumed to be 15 ml. Unless otherwise stated, milk is assumed to be full fat, eggs and individual vegetables are medium, and pepper is freshly ground black pepper. Unless otherwise stated, all root vegetables should be peeled prior to using.

Garnishes, decorations and serving suggestions are all optional and not necessarily included in the recipe ingredients or method. Any optional ingredients and seasoning to taste are not included in the nutritional analysis. The times given are an approximate guide only. Preparation times differ according to the techniques used by different people and the cooking times may also vary from those given. Optional ingredients, variations or serving suggestions have not been included in the time calculations. Nutritional values are per serving (Serves...) or per item (Makes...).

While the author has made all reasonable efforts to ensure that the information contained in this book is accurate and up to date at the time of publication, anyone reading this book should note the following important points:-

Medical and pharmaceutical knowledge is constantly changing and the author and the publisher cannot and do not guarantee the accuracy or appropriateness of the contents of this book; In any event, this book is not intended to be, and should not be relied upon, as a substitute for appropriate, tailored professional advice. Both the author and the publisher strongly recommend that a doctor or other healthcare professional is consulted before embarking on major dietary changes; For the reasons set out above, and to the fullest extent permitted by law, the author and publisher: (i) cannot and do not accept any legal duty of care or responsibility in relation to the accuracy or appropriateness of the contents of this book, even where expressed as 'advice' or using other words to this effect; and (ii) disclaim any liability, loss, damage or risk that may be claimed or incurred as a consequence – directly or indirectly – of the use and/or application of any of the contents of this book.

contents

breakfast & brunch   6

snacks & lunches   44

dinnertime feasts   80

super sides & breads   118

baking & desserts   154

index   192

let's do brunch!

When people think of breakfast or brunch, most would imagine it hard to avoid eating dairy or gluten, with milk and cereals being popular breakfast staples. But it's easy to create varied and delicious breakfasts for allergy sufferers — eggs, fruit, grains and seeds all make great bases for breakfasts.

breakfast & brunch

kiwi quencher juice → 8
berry sunrise smoothie → 10
strawberry & vanilla soya shake → 12
millet porridge with apricot topping → 14
raw buckwheat & almond porridge → 16
apple & seed muesli → 18
fruit compote with quinoa → 20
apricot & raisin oat bars → 22
honey & blueberry bars → 24
ALLERGIES AND INTOLERANCES → 26
breakfast cookies → 28
herby tofu scramble → 30
potato & onion frittata → 32
red beetroot hash → 34
sausage & potato omelette → 36
eggs in pepper & tomato sauce → 38
courgette loaf → 40
banana & brazil nut loaf → 42

kiwi quencher juice

½ romaine lettuce
4 kiwi fruits, peeled
115 g/4 oz green grapes
1 large pear, halved
small handful of ice, to serve (optional)

1. Peel off a lettuce leaf and reserve.

2. Feed the kiwi fruits and grapes, then the lettuce and pear through a juicer. Half-fill a glass with ice (if using), then pour in the juice.

3. Decorate the juice with the reserved lettuce leaf and serve immediately.

fact

This is a great juice for rehydrating first thing in the morning. The grapes are naturally juicy and the lettuce is thirst quenching.

cals: 414   fat: 2.5g   sat fat: 0.2g   fibre: 20.6g   carbs: 103.5g   sugar: 67.5g   salt: trace   protein: 7.3g

berry sunrise smoothie

prep: 10–15 mins
cook: no cooking

1 banana
55 g/2 oz silken plain tofu, drained
175 ml/6 fl oz pure orange juice
200 g/7 oz frozen mixed berries

1. Roughly chop the banana and the tofu into smaller pieces.

2. Place all of the ingredients into a food processor or blender, or place into a large, deep bowl and use a hand-held blender.

3. Blend gently until thoroughly combined.

4. Serve immediately in a tall drinking glass.

fact

This smoothie is a good way to start the day as the fruit provides vital vitamins and minerals and the tofu provides essential protein.

cals: 282   fat: 2.6g   sat fat: 0.3g   fibre: 6.6g   carbs: 60g   sugar: 42.8g   salt: trace   protein: 6.5g

strawberry & vanilla soya shake

prep: 10-15 mins
cook: no cooking

200 g/7 oz strawberries
200 ml/7 fl oz plain soya yogurt
100 ml/3½ fl oz chilled soya milk
2 tsp vanilla extract
agave nectar, to taste

fact

Soya milk makes a good alternative to cow's milk as it contains less fat but contains similar amounts of protein. It also contains essential fatty acids.

1. Pick over the strawberries, then hull and halve them and place into a small bowl.

2. Place the strawberry halves, yogurt, milk and vanilla extract into a food processor or blender, or place these ingredients into a large, deep bowl and use a hand-held blender. Blend gently until thoroughly combined. Sweeten with agave nectar to taste.

3. Serve immediately in tall drinking glasses.

cals: 151   fat: 2.8g   sat fat: 0.3g   fibre: 0.8g   carbs: 24.6g   sugar: 16.7g   salt: trace   protein: 4.7g

millet porridge with apricot topping

prep: 15-20 mins
cook: 35 mins

225 g/8 oz millet flakes
900 ml/1½ pints soya milk
pinch of salt
freshly grated nutmeg, to serve

apricot topping
115 g/4 oz ready-to-eat dried apricots,
  roughly chopped
300 ml/10 fl oz water

1. To make the apricot topping, put the apricots into a saucepan and cover with the water. Bring to the boil, then reduce the heat and simmer, half covered, for 20 minutes until the apricots are very tender. Use a hand-held blender or transfer the apricots, along with any water left in the saucepan, to a blender and process until smooth. Set aside.

2. To make the porridge, put the millet flakes into a saucepan and add the milk and salt. Bring to the boil, then reduce the heat and simmer for 5 minutes, stirring frequently, until cooked and creamy.

3. Transfer the apricot topping to a serving bowl. To serve, spoon the porridge into four bowls and top each bowl with the apricot and a little nutmeg.

top tip

Millet flakes are a good way to make a substantial porridge that doesn't contain gluten.

raw buckwheat & almond porridge

prep: 25 mins, plus soaking and chilling
cook: no cooking

almond milk

70 g/2½ oz whole raw almonds,
  soaked overnight in water

300 ml/10 fl oz water

porridge

350 g/12 oz raw buckwheat groats,
  soaked in cold water for 90 minutes

1 tsp cinnamon

2 tbsp light agave nectar,
  plus extra to serve

sliced strawberries, to serve (optional)

1. To make the almond milk, drain the almonds and transfer to a blender or food processor. Blend the almonds with the water. Blend for a minute or two to break down the almonds as much as possible.

2. Pour the mixture into a sieve lined with muslin and squeeze through as much of the liquid as possible into a large bowl or jug. You should get approximately 300 ml/10 fl oz of raw almond milk.

3. Rinse the soaked buckwheat thoroughly in cold water. Transfer to the blender or food processor with the almond milk, cinnamon and agave nectar. Blend the mixture to a slightly coarse texture.

4. Chill the mixture for at least 30 minutes or overnight. It can be stored, covered, in the refrigerator for 3 days.

5. Serve in small bowls, topped with strawberries and agave nectar to taste.

serves 6

variation

If you can't find agave nectar, then any type of honey or maple syrup is fine to use too.

cals: 227   fat: 2.5g   sat fat: 0.9g   fibre: 6.2g   carbs: 47.6g   sugar: 5.3g   salt: 0.1g   protein: 7.9g

apple & seed muesli

prep: 15 mins, plus cooling
cook: 5 mins

75 g/2¾ oz sunflower seeds

50 g/1¾ oz pumpkin seeds

90 g/3¼ oz hazelnuts, roughly chopped

125 g/4½ oz buckwheat flakes

125 g/4½ oz rice flakes

125 g/4½ oz millet flakes

115 g/4 oz ready-to-eat dried apple, roughly chopped

115 g/4 oz ready-to-eat dried dates, stoned and roughly chopped

1. Place a frying pan over a medium heat. Add the sunflower seeds, pumpkin seeds and hazelnuts and toast, shaking the frying pan frequently for 4 minutes, or until they are golden brown.

2. Transfer the seed mixture to a large bowl and leave to cool.

3. Add the buckwheat flakes, rice flakes, millet flakes, dried apple and dates to the bowl and mix well.

4. Serve immediately or store in an airtight container for up to five days.

3

fact

Buckwheat is a seed, although many people mistakenly think of it as a grain. It is a nutrition powerhouse, containing lots of protein. It is also a good source of fibre.

fruit compote with quinoa

prep: 20 mins
cook: 15 mins, plus standing

75 g/2¾ oz white quinoa, rinsed

500 ml/17 fl oz water

2 tsp honey, plus extra to serve

pinch of freshly grated nutmeg

finely grated rind of 1 small orange

10 ready-to-eat dried apricots

6 ready-to-eat prunes,
   stoned

20 g/¾ oz dried apple rings, halved

4 tbsp dried cranberries

2 tbsp coconut chips

1. Put the quinoa into a medium-sized saucepan with 225 ml/8 fl oz of the water. Add the honey, nutmeg and half of the orange rind.

2. Bring to the boil, then cover and simmer over a very low heat for 10 minutes, or until most of the liquid has evaporated. Remove from the heat, but leave the pan covered for a further 7 minutes to allow the grains to swell. Fluff up with a fork.

3. Meanwhile, put the apricots, prunes, apple rings and cranberries into a separate saucepan. Add the remaining water and orange rind.

4. Bring to the boil, then simmer over a medium heat for 4–5 minutes, until the fruit is soft. Drain, reserving the liquid.

5. Divide the quinoa between two bowls. Spoon the fruit over the top and pour over the cooking liquid. Sprinkle with the coconut chips and serve immediately.

serves 2

variation

To give a more tropical taste, replace the dried prunes with dried pineapple.

cals: 414   fat: 4.6g   sat fat: 1.8g   fibre: 9g   carbs: 86.6g   sugar: 48.7g   salt: trace   protein: 6.9g

apricot & raisin oat bars

prep: 25 mins, plus cooling
cook: 45-50 mins

350 g/12 oz ready-to-eat
  dried apricots

2 tbsp sunflower oil, plus extra
  for oiling

finely grated rind of ½ orange

seeds from 5 cardamom pods,
  crushed (optional)

140 g/5 oz raisins

115 g/4 oz gluten-free rolled oats

1. Put the apricots into a saucepan with enough water to cover. Cook over a medium heat until almost boiling, then reduce the heat and simmer for 5 minutes, or until completely soft. Drain.

2. Put the apricots into a food processor with the 2 tablespoons of oil and purée.

3. Tip the purée into a bowl and stir in the orange rind and the cardamom seeds, if using. Leave to cool.

4. Preheat the oven to 180°C/350°F/Gas Mark 4. Brush a 20-cm/8-inch square baking tin with oil.

5. Stir the raisins and oats into the apricot mixture. Spread out in the prepared tin, levelling the surface with a spatula.

6. Bake in the preheated oven for 35–40 minutes, until firm. Cover with foil after about 25 minutes to prevent burning.

7. Leave to cool in the tin for 15 minutes. Turn out onto a wire rack and leave to cool completely before cutting into bars.

makes 12

top tip

The oats in this breakfast bar help to make this a filling start to the day.

cals: 162   fat: 3.1g   sat fat: 0.4g   fibre: 3.6g   carbs: 34.1g   sugar: 22.7g   salt: trace   protein: 2.6g

honey & blueberry bars

prep: 20 mins, plus cooling
cook: 30-35 mins

sunflower oil, for oiling
85 g/3 oz gluten-free self-raising flour
55 g/2 oz quinoa flakes
55 g/2 oz puffed rice
55 g/2 oz flaked almonds
225 g/8 oz blueberries
100 g/3½ oz dairy-free spread
100 g/3½ oz honey
1 egg, beaten

1. Preheat the oven to 180°C/350°F/
Gas Mark 4. Brush a shallow 28 x 18-cm/
11 x 7-inch baking tin with oil and line the
base with baking paper.

2. Mix together the flour, quinoa, puffed rice,
almonds and blueberries. Place the spread and
honey in a pan and heat gently until melted,
then stir evenly into the dry ingredients with
the egg.

3. Spread out the mixture in the prepared tin,
levelling the surface with a spatula. Bake in
the preheated oven for 25–30 minutes, until
golden brown and firm.

4. Leave to cool in the tin for 15 minutes, then
cut into 12 bars. Transfer the bars to a wire
rack to cool completely.

fact

Blueberries are packed with antioxidants that
support your immune system and contain lots of
vitamin C.

cals: 183   fat: 9.4g   sat fat: 1.7g   fibre: 1.5g   carbs: 22.9g   sugar: 9.2g   salt: 0.1g   protein: 3g

allergies and intolerances

A diagnosis of food allergy or intolerance need not cause the drastic changes to your diet that you may imagine. You'll need to be more careful in selecting foods and take care to study labels thoroughly, but this soon becomes second nature and once accustomed to the changes you'll see the benefits of a healthier diet.

allergy free

Allergy or intolerance?

There is some confusion between food allergy and intolerance, so it's important to establish which applies to you. A food allergy occurs when a food triggers the body's immune system to react adversely, usually within minutes. Once the immune system has been primed to produce these abnormal antibodies, the symptoms may be amplified the next time, causing severe allergic reactions to develop even with slight exposure. Most adverse reactions to foods are caused by intolerances. These usually occur when the body's digestive system is unable to digest foods properly, and the reactions are slower and less severe. Our bodies usually adapt to cope with a wide variety of foods, but when under stress, then intolerances may develop.

Coeliac disease

Coeliac disease is an auto-immune disease, which occurs when the body's immune system reacts abnormally to gluten, the protein in wheat, barley and rye, and produces antibodies that attack its own tissues. This causes inflammation and damage to the lining of the small intestine, which reduces the body's ability to absorb nutrients, causing symptoms such as diarrhoea, stomach pain and bloating and anaemia. If left untreated it can lead to problems like osteoporosis, miscarriage, depression and infertility. A blood test and biopsy can diagnose coeliac disease, and a doctor or dietitian will advise on a strict gluten-free diet. Once foods containing gluten are removed from the diet, the damaged intestinal lining can recover and function properly, but coeliac disease is a lifetime condition so you will need to restrict your diet permanently.

Wheat intolerence

Wheat allergy or intolerance can cause varied symptoms, including sinusitis (swelling of the sinuses), asthma, itchy and sore eyes, earache, headaches, migraine, muscle pain, stomach cramps, skin rashes, mouth ulcers, coughing, tiredness, depression, bloating, flatulence and nausea. Diagnosis involves blood and skin tests, but these are not always 100% reliable so a strict exclusion diet is the best way to diagnose the problem.

Dairy intolerance

A dairy sensitivity can be the result of an intolerance caused by an inability to digest lactose, a natural sugar in milk, or by an allergy to the protein in milk. Lactose intolerance can occur at any age and can be permanent or temporary. Dairy allergies often start in childhood, but children may grow out of it. Symptoms vary, but include asthma, eczema, sinus problems, bloating, stomach pain and digestive problems. Depending on the suspected cause, a blood, skin or ingestion test is used for diagnosis, and treatment is by exclusion diet.

Don't miss out on nutrients

It's important to consult a doctor before restricting your diet, and it's vital to ensure that you get all the essential nutrients by eating a good balance of food types.

breakfast cookies

prep: 20-25 mins, plus cooling
cook: 12-15 mins

sunflower oil, for greasing

115 g/4 oz Brazil nuts

85 g/3 oz gluten-free icing sugar

100 g/3½ oz buckwheat flour

½ tsp gluten-free baking powder

½ tsp xanthan gum

85 g/3 oz sultanas

25 g/1 oz desiccated coconut

2 egg whites

poppy seeds and dark muscovado
sugar, to sprinkle

1. Preheat the oven to 180°C/350°F/Gas Mark 4. Lightly grease a large baking sheet.

2. Place the Brazil nuts, icing sugar and buckwheat flour in a food processor and process until finely ground.

3. Transfer the mixture to a large bowl then stir in the baking powder and xanthan gum.

4. Stir in the sultanas, coconut and egg whites and combine thoroughly using your hands, until a soft, sticky dough forms.

5. Divide the mixture into six and roll each piece into a ball. Place on the prepared baking sheet and press each ball with your fingers to create 12-cm/4½-inch rounds. Sprinkle lightly with poppy seeds and muscovado sugar.

6. Bake in the preheated oven for 12–15 minutes, or until firm and just beginning to brown. Leave to cool on the baking sheet before serving.

makes 6

variation

For a change of flavour, replace the sultanas with an equal amount of chopped dried apricots.

cals: 345   fat: 17.8g   sat fat: 5.6g   fibre: 4.7g   carbs: 42g   sugar: 25g   salt: 0.5g   protein: 7.1g

herby tofu scramble

prep: 20 mins
cook: 15 mins

400 g/14 oz firm plain tofu, drained
   and dried
12 cherry tomatoes on the vine
olive oil, for roasting
1 large gluten-free and dairy-free roll
30 g/1 oz dairy-free spread
2 garlic cloves, halved and bruised
5 tbsp chopped fresh mixed herbs
salt and pepper
smoked paprika, to taste

1. Preheat the oven to 200°C/400°F/Gas
Mark 6. Gently crumble the tofu into a
large bowl.

2. Place the tomatoes in a roasting tin and
drizzle lightly with olive oil. Roast for 5
minutes, or until beginning to split.

3. Cut the roll in half and slice each half
lengthways. Lightly toast the bread slices.

4. Melt the spread in a large frying pan over a
medium heat. Sauté the garlic in the spread
for 1 minute, then remove the garlic from the
pan and discard.

5. Put the tofu into the frying pan and fry it in
the garlic-infused oil, turning occasionally, for
3–4 minutes, or until just browning. Remove
from the heat, stir in the fresh chopped herbs,
and add salt and pepper to taste.

6. Sprinkle the tofu scramble with smoked
paprika to taste. Serve the scramble
immediately on the toasted roll, with the
roasted tomatoes on the side.

serves 2

top tip

If you can find a gluten and dairy-free ciabatta roll, this would work well in this recipe.

cals: 416   fat: 23.2g   sat fat: 3.9g   fibre: 5.4g   carbs: 34.7g   sugar: 7.6g   salt: 2.2g   protein: 17.7g

potato & onion frittata

prep: 25 mins
cook: 50 mins

4 tbsp olive oil

2 large onions, halved and thinly sliced

125 ml/4 fl oz water

50 g/1¾ oz red quinoa, rinsed

700 g/1 lb 9 oz waxy potatoes, peeled, halved lengthways and thinly sliced

9 eggs

½ tsp dried oregano

½ tsp salt

¼ tsp pepper

fact

Quinoa is said to be the only plant food that contains all nine essential amino acids, putting it on a par with animal protein. It is also naturally gluten free.

1. Heat the oil in a frying pan, add the onions and gently fry over a low–medium heat for 25 minutes, until golden and very soft. Drain the onions, reserving the oil.

2. Meanwhile, put the water and quinoa into a small saucepan and bring to the boil. Cover and simmer over a very low heat for 10 minutes, or until most of the liquid has evaporated. Remove from the heat, but leave the pan covered for a further 10 minutes to allow the grains to swell. Fluff up with a fork.

3. While the quinoa is cooking, put the potatoes in a steamer and steam for 8 minutes, until just tender. Spread out to dry on a clean tea towel.

4. Beat the eggs with the oregano, salt and pepper. Stir the onions, potatoes and quinoa into the egg mixture.

5. Heat the reserved oil in a deep 25-cm/ 10-inch non-stick frying pan with a heatproof handle. Pour in the egg mixture, cover and cook over a low–medium heat for 15 minutes. Meanwhile, preheat the grill.

6. Place the pan under the preheated grill for 5 minutes to finish cooking the top of the frittata. Turn out onto a plate, cut into wedges and serve immediately.

cals: 536   fat: 26.5g   sat fat: 5.9g   fibre: 5.7g   carbs: 53.4g   sugar: 6.2g   salt: 1.2g   protein: 21.7g

red beetroot hash

prep: 30 mins
cook: 45 mins

350 g/12 oz Jerusalem artichokes, unpeeled and scrubbed

450 g/1 lb raw beetroot, cut into cubes

750 g/1 lb 10 oz sweet potatoes, cut into cubes

2 tbsp olive oil

1 red onion, roughly chopped

2 tsp mild paprika

½ tsp mustard powder

3 tsp fresh thyme, plus extra to garnish

4 eggs

salt and pepper

fact

Knobbly-looking Jerusalem artichokes are considered to help digestion. What's more, they're packed with fibre, helping you to feel fuller for longer.

1. Halve any of the larger artichokes. Half-fill the base of a steamer with water, bring to the boil, then add the artichokes to the water. Put the beetroot in one half of the steamer top, cover with a lid and steam for 10 minutes. Put the sweet potatoes in the other half of the top, so the colour of the beetroot won't bleed into the sweet potatoes.

2. Cover with a lid again and steam for 10 minutes more, or until all the vegetables are just tender. Drain the artichokes, peel them and cut them into cubes.

3. Heat 1 tablespoon of oil in a frying pan over a medium heat. Add the red onion and fry for 3–4 minutes, or until beginning to soften. Add the artichokes, beetroot and sweet potatoes and fry for 10 minutes, or until browned.

4. Stir in the paprika, mustard powder and thyme and season well with salt and pepper. Make four spaces in the frying pan, drizzle in the remaining oil, then crack an egg into each hole. Sprinkle the eggs with salt and pepper, then cover and cook for 4–5 minutes, or until the eggs are cooked to your liking.

5. Spoon onto plates and serve immediately, garnished with extra thyme.

serves 4

cals: 434   fat: 12.6g   sat fat: 2.7g   fibre: 11.6g   carbs: 68.1g   sugar: 26.1g   salt: 1.4g   protein: 14.2g

sausage & potato omelette

prep: 20 mins, plus cooling
cook: 18-21 mins

4 gluten and dairy-free sausages
  (meat or vegetarian)
sunflower oil, for frying
4 boiled potatoes, cooled and diced
8 cherry tomatoes
4 eggs, beaten
salt and pepper

1. Preheat the grill to medium–high. Arrange the sausages on a foil-lined grill pan and cook under the preheated grill, turning occasionally, for 12–15 minutes, or until cooked through and golden brown. Leave to cool slightly, then slice into bite-sized pieces.

2. Meanwhile, heat a little oil in a large, non-stick frying pan with a heatproof handle over a medium heat. Add the potatoes and cook until golden brown and crisp all over, then add the tomatoes and cook for a further 2 minutes. Arrange the sausages in the pan so that there is an even distribution of potatoes, tomatoes and sausages.

3. Add a little more oil to the pan if it seems dry. Season the beaten eggs to taste and pour the mixture over the ingredients in the pan. Cook for 3 minutes, without stirring or disturbing the eggs. Place the pan under the preheated grill for 3 minutes, or until the top is just cooked. Cut into wedges to serve.

serves 4

variation

Try replacing the sausage with chopped mushrooms or shredded spinach.

cals: 391   fat: 23.9g   sat fat: 7.3g   fibre: 2.1g   carbs: 25.1g   sugar: 2.8g   salt: 2.7g   protein: 19.8g

eggs in pepper & tomato sauce

prep: 20 mins
cook: 30 mins

4 large tomatoes

1½ tbsp rapeseed oil

1 large onion, finely chopped

½ tsp coriander seeds, crushed

½ tsp caraway seeds, crushed

2 red peppers, deseeded and roughly chopped

¼ tsp dried red chilli flakes

1 large garlic clove, thinly sliced

4 eggs

salt and pepper

1 tbsp roughly chopped fresh flat-leaf parsley, to garnish

1. Put the tomatoes in a shallow bowl and cover with boiling water. Leave for 30 seconds, then drain. Slip off the skins and discard, then chop the tomatoes.

2. Heat the oil in a large frying pan over a medium heat. Add the onion, coriander seeds and caraway seeds. Fry, stirring occasionally, for 10 minutes, or until the onion is soft and golden.

3. Stir in the red peppers and chilli flakes and fry for 5 minutes more, or until softened. Add the garlic and tomatoes and season with salt and pepper. Reduce the heat to low and simmer, uncovered, for 10 minutes.

4. Crack the eggs over the surface. Cover and cook for a further 4–5 minutes, or until the eggs are cooked to your liking. Season with salt and pepper, sprinkle with the parsley and serve immediately.

4

fact

Tomatoes contain vitamins A, C and E, as well as zinc and selenium, all of which can help fight harmful free radicals.

cals: 189   fat: 11.2g   sat fat: 2.1g   fibre: 3.8g   carbs: 13.7g   sugar: 7.5g   salt: 1.7g   protein: 9.2g

courgette loaf

prep: 25 mins, plus cooling
cook: 55–60 mins

oil, for greasing

380 g/13½ oz gluten-free plain flour

1 tsp gluten-free baking powder

2 tsp xanthan gum

1 tsp gluten-free bicarbonate of soda

1 tsp mixed spice

2 tsp cinnamon

225 g/8 oz caster sugar

3 eggs

240 ml/8½ fl oz vegetable oil

2 tsp vanilla extract

115 g/4 oz walnuts, roughly chopped

220 g/7¾ oz courgettes,
  finely grated

top tip

This tasty, healthy loaf, packed with vegetables and nuts, makes a better-for-you alternative to plain white bread. Serve with dairy-free spread.

1. Preheat the oven to 160°C/325°F/Gas Mark 3. Grease two 450-g/1-lb loaf tins and line with baking paper.

2. Sift the flour, baking powder, xanthan gum, bicarbonate of soda and spices together into a large bowl.

3. In a separate bowl, whisk the sugar, eggs, vegetable oil and vanilla extract until a creamy consistency forms. Add the flour mixture, walnuts and courgettes to the bowl and fold in to make a smooth batter.

4. Divide the mixture between the two tins and bake in the preheated oven for 55–60 minutes, or until firm to the touch.

5. Leave to cool in the tins for approximately 20 minutes before transferring to a wire rack to cool. Leave the bread to rest on the rack for at least 30 minutes before serving.

cals: 2741   fat: 172.7   sat fat: 19.2g   fibre: 8.4g   carbs: 279.8g   sugar: 118.4g   salt: 2.5g   protein: 29.8g

banana & brazil nut loaf

prep: 25 mins, plus cooling
cook: 45-50 mins

55 g/2 oz soya flour
55 g/2 oz gluten-free cornflour
70 g/2½ oz tapioca flour
2 tsp gluten-free baking powder
½ tsp xanthan gum
2 tsp mixed spice
85 g/3 oz light muscovado sugar
2 eggs, beaten
1 tsp vanilla extract
4 tbsp sunflower oil, plus extra for greasing
3 very ripe bananas, mashed
100 g/3½ oz Brazil nuts, chopped

1. Grease a 900-g/2-lb loaf tin with oil and line with baking paper. Preheat the oven to 180°C/350°F/Gas Mark 4.

2. Sift the soya flour, cornflour, tapioca flour, baking powder, xanthan gum and mixed spice together into a bowl and add the sugar, eggs, vanilla extract, oil and bananas. Beat well with a wooden spoon or an electric whisk until a thick batter forms.

3. Fold in the chopped nuts and spoon the mixture into the prepared tin. Bake the loaf in the preheated oven for 45–50 minutes, or until golden brown and firm.

4. Leave to cool in the tin for 10 minutes, then turn out and transfer to a wire rack to cool completely.

fact

Bananas provide good levels of potassium and are used by athletes to maintain energy levels. They also contain good levels of fibre.

cals: 2782   fat: 148.1g   sat fat: 26.5g   fibre: 23.3g   carbs: 310.7g   sugar: 144.8g   salt: 4g   protein: 51.6g

Grazing and power snacks are becoming increasingly popular ways of trying to eat healthily and reduce your calorie intake during the day. For intolerance sufferers, there are lots of ways to enjoy tasty snacks – seeds, nuts and fruit are all fine to eat so you can enjoy varied daytime treats between meals, as shown in this chapter.

snacks & lunches

date & seed power balls 46

fruit, nut & seed trail mix 48

sweet potato chips 50

salsa bean dip 52

cracker bites 54

nutty toffee popcorn 56

green lentil & vegetable soup 58

crab & ginger soup 60

warm chicken & mango salad 62

DAIRY-FREE ALTERNATIVES 64

seared beef salad 66

shaker salad in a jar 68

polenta bruschettas with tapenade 70

easy vegetable sushi 72

monkfish ceviche with red quinoa 74

chicken balls with dipping sauce 76

vietnamese tofu & noodle salad 78

date & seed power balls

prep: 30–35 mins, plus chilling
cook: no cooking

85 g/3 oz gluten and dairy-free plain chocolate

40 g/1½ oz sunflower seeds

40 g/1½ oz linseeds

40 g/1½ oz sesame seeds

100 g/3½ oz Brazil nuts, roughly chopped

140 g/5 oz Medjool dates, stoned

40 g/1½ oz goji berries

1 tsp ground cinnamon

1 tbsp natural maca powder

40 g/1½ oz unsweetened desiccated coconut

6 tbsp maple syrup

1. Break 55 g/2 oz chocolate into pieces and reserve the rest. Put the sunflower seeds, linseeds, sesame seeds, Brazil nuts and chocolate in a food processor and process until finely ground, scraping down the sides of the processor once or twice.

2. Add the dates, goji berries, cinnamon, maca and 25 g/1 oz coconut, then spoon in the maple syrup. Process until you have a coarse paste.

3. Using a measuring spoon, scoop out tablespoons of the mixture onto a plate, then adjust the sizes of the mounds to make 20. Roll them into balls.

4. Put the remaining coconut on one plate and finely grate the remaining chocolate onto another plate. Roll half the balls in the coconut and the rest in the chocolate. Pack into an airtight container and store in the fridge for up to three days.

makes 20

cals: 253   fat: 9.4g   sat fat: 3.2g   fibre: 3g   carbs: 15.7g   sugar: 9.4g   salt: trace   protein: 2.9g

fruit, nut & seed trail mix

prep: 20 mins, plus cooling
cook: 8-10 mins

200 g/7 oz whole unblanched almonds

25 g/1 oz pine nuts

25 g/1 oz pumpkin seeds

25 g/1 oz sunflower seeds

25 g/1 oz dried banana chips

55 g/2 oz dates, stoned and roughly chopped

2 tbsp gluten-free porridge oats

½ tsp ground mixed spice

1 small egg white

1. Preheat the oven to 200°C/400°F/Gas Mark 6. Combine the almonds, pine nuts, pumpkin and sunflower seeds, banana chips, dates, oats and spice in a large bowl and mix well.

2. Lightly beat the egg white with a fork in a small bowl, then add to the nut mixture in the bowl, stirring to coat all the ingredients evenly.

3. Spread the mixture out on a large baking tray in a single layer. Bake in the preheated oven for 8–10 minutes, or until crisp and lightly browned.

4. Leave to cool completely before serving or pack into an airtight container and consume within five days.

variation

Replace the banana, date and spice with 1 tsp gluten-free curry powder and ¼ tsp salt.

cals: 75   fat: 5.7g   sat fat: 0.5g   fibre: 1.4g   carbs: 4.7g   sugar: 2.1g   salt: trace   protein: 2.6g

sweet potato chips

prep: 20 mins
cook: 15–20 mins

2 sprays of vegetable oil spray
900 g/2 lb sweet potatoes
½ tsp salt
½ tsp ground cumin
¼ tsp cayenne pepper

1. Preheat the oven to 230°C/450°F/Gas Mark 8. Spray a large baking tray with vegetable oil spray.

2. Peel the sweet potatoes and slice into 5-mm/¼-inch thick spears about 7.5 cm/ 3 inches long. Spread the sweet potatoes on the prepared baking tray and spray them with vegetable oil spray.

3. In a small bowl, combine the salt, cumin and cayenne pepper. Sprinkle the spice mixture evenly over the sweet potatoes and then toss to coat.

4. Spread the sweet potatoes out into a single layer and bake in the preheated oven for about 15–20 minutes, or until cooked through and lightly coloured. Serve hot.

serves 4

variation

Instead of the salt, cumin and cayenne, you can use a teaspoon of gluten-free Cajun seasoning.

cals: 176   fat: 0.3g   sat fat: trace   fibre: 6.8g   carbs: 45.3g   sugar: 9.4g   salt: 1g   protein: 3.6g

salsa bean dip

prep: 20-25 mins, plus chilling and cooling
cook: 5 mins

200 g/7 oz cherry tomatoes, quartered

1 small red onion, very finely chopped

200 g/7 oz canned aduki beans, drained and rinsed

½ red pepper, deseeded and finely chopped

½ or 1 red chilli (to taste), deseeded and very finely chopped

2 tsp sun-dried tomato purée

1 tsp honey

large handful of chopped fresh coriander

salt and pepper

chilli oil, to serve (optional)

4 gluten-free tortillas, to serve (optional)

1. Place the tomatoes, onion, beans, red pepper, chilli, purée, honey and coriander in a large bowl. Mix together well and season to taste with salt and pepper.

2. Cover the bowl and leave in the refrigerator for at least 15 minutes to let the flavours develop. Preheat the grill to medium.

3. Place the tortillas under the preheated grill and lightly toast. Leave to cool slightly then cut into slices.

4. Transfer the bean dip to a small serving bowl. Serve with the sliced tortillas and chilli oil to dip.

fact

Aduki beans are a small, reddish-brown bean with a nutty flavour. They are popular in Asian cuisine and are said to be good for the liver.

cals: 80   fat: 1.1g   sat fat: 0.3g   fibre: 3g   carbs: 14g   sugar: 5.1g   salt: 1.5g   protein: 3.5g

cracker bites

prep: 25 mins, plus cooling
cook: 15–18 mins

175 g/6 oz gluten-free plain flour,
plus extra for dusting
30 g/1 oz nutritional yeast flakes
1 tsp dried thyme
3 tbsp rapeseed oil
salt and pepper

1. Preheat the oven to 180°C/350°F/Gas Mark 4. Cover a large baking sheet with baking paper.

2. Put the flour, yeast flakes and thyme into a large mixing bowl and season to taste. Stir with a wooden spoon to combine.

3. Stir in the oil and gradually add 6–7 tablespoons of cold water. Use your hands to bring the mixture together to form a dough that is soft but not sticky.

4. Turn the dough out onto a lightly floured board and roll it to around 3 mm/⅛ inch thick. Use a small cookie cutter (2.5–5 cm/ 1–2 inches in diameter) to cut out the crackers and place them on the prepared baking sheet. Re-roll the dough trimmings and make as many crackers as you can.

5. Bake in the preheated oven for 15–18 minutes, or until just golden on the bottom. Leave the crackers to cool on the baking sheet for a few minutes, then use a palette knife to transfer them to a wire rack to cool.

top tip

These crackers taste great when served with dairy-free cheeses and pickles.

nutty toffee popcorn

prep: 15-20 mins, plus cooling
cook: 10-15 mins

40 g/1½ oz dairy-free spread
40 g/1½ oz brown sugar
1 tbsp golden syrup
70 g/2½ oz cashew nuts
50 g/1¾ oz popping corn
1 tbsp vegetable oil

1. Place the spread, sugar and golden syrup in a saucepan over a medium heat. Bring the temperature up to high and stir continuously for 2 minutes, then remove from the heat and set aside.

2. Toast the cashew nuts in a dry, heavy-based pan over a medium heat for 3–4 minutes, stirring frequently, until they begin to turn golden brown. Remove from the heat and transfer to a plate.

3. In a large, lidded saucepan, stir the popping corn together with the oil until it is well coated. Put the lid on the pan and place over a medium heat. Listen for popping and turn the heat to low. Shake the pan occasionally, holding the lid down firmly. Do not lift the lid until the popping has finished.

4. While the popcorn is still warm, stir in the toasted cashews. Pour over the toffee sauce and stir well to coat the popcorn. Transfer the popcorn to a baking sheet lined with baking paper and allow to cool before serving.

fact

Popping corn is a delicious treat that is naturally gluten free! The addition of cashews adds protein.

cals: 601   fat: 42.2g   sat fat: 7.2g   fibre: 3.8g   carbs: 49.6g   sugar: 28.2   salt: 0.1g   protein: 8.6g

green lentil & vegetable soup

prep: 20-25 mins
cook: 1¼ hours-1 hour 25 mins

3 tbsp olive oil

1 Spanish onion, chopped

3 garlic cloves, chopped

2 celery sticks, chopped

1 carrot, chopped

1 potato, chopped

175 g/6 oz smoked ham, chopped

450 g/1 lb green or brown lentils

3 litres/5¼ pints gluten-free stock

1 bay leaf

4 fresh parsley sprigs

4 tomatoes, peeled and chopped

1½ tsp sweet paprika

4 tbsp gluten-free sherry vinegar

salt and pepper

1. Heat the oil in a large saucepan. Add the onion, garlic, celery, carrot and potato and cook over a low heat, stirring occasionally, for 5–7 minutes, until softened.

2. Add the ham and cook, stirring occasionally, for a further 3 minutes. Remove the vegetables and ham from the pan and set aside.

3. Add the lentils, stock, bay leaf and parsley to the pan, increase the heat to medium and bring to the boil. Reduce the heat and simmer, stirring occasionally, for 30 minutes.

4. Add the tomatoes and return the vegetables and ham to the pan. Stir well and simmer for 25–30 minutes more.

5. Remove and discard the bay leaf and parsley. Stir in the paprika and vinegar, season to taste with salt and pepper and heat through for 2–3 minutes. Ladle into warmed soup bowls and serve immediately.

cals: 461   fat: 12.2g   sat fat: 3g   fibre: 26.1g   carbs: 57.5g   sugar: 6.3g   salt: 6.4g   protein: 29.6g

crab & ginger soup

prep: 20 mins
cook: 35 mins

2 tbsp chilli oil

1 garlic clove, chopped

4 spring onions, trimmed and sliced

2 red peppers, deseeded and chopped

1 tbsp grated fresh ginger

1 litre/1¾ pints gluten-free fish stock

100 ml/3½ fl oz coconut milk

100 ml/3½ fl oz rice wine

2 tbsp lime juice

1 tbsp grated lime rind

6 young kaffir lime leaves, finely shredded

300 g/10½ oz freshly cooked crabmeat

200 g/7 oz freshly cooked crab claws

150 g/5½ oz canned sweetcorn, drained

1 tbsp chopped fresh coriander, plus a few sprigs to garnish

salt and pepper

fact

This delicious Thai-inspired soup contains sweet coconut milk which is offset perfectly by the aromatic ginger and zingy lime juice.

1. Heat the oil in a large saucepan. Add the garlic and spring onions and cook, stirring for about 3 minutes, until slightly softened. Add the peppers and ginger and cook for a further 4 minutes, stirring.

2. Pour in the stock and season with salt and pepper. Bring to the boil, then reduce the heat.

3. Pour in the coconut milk, rice wine and lime juice, and stir in the grated lime rind and kaffir lime leaves. Leave to simmer for 15 minutes.

4. Add the crabmeat and crab claws to the soup with the corn and coriander. Cook for 5 minutes, or until the crab is heated through.

5. Ladle into warmed soup bowls, garnish with coriander and serve immediately.

cals: 305   fat: 15.5g   sat fat: 7.1g   fibre: 3.1g   carbs: 15.4g   sugar: 3g   salt: 6g   protein: 25.4g

warm chicken & mango salad

prep: 20 mins
cook: 10 mins

1 tbsp groundnut oil
600 g/1 lb 5 oz chicken breast, sliced
280 g/10 oz green beans, sliced
280 g/10 oz Chinese leaves, shredded
85 g/3 oz salted peanuts, chopped
4 tbsp chopped fresh coriander
1 mango, stoned and diced

dressing
2 tbsp gluten-free Thai fish sauce
1 tbsp clear honey
4 tbsp lemon juice
1 red chilli, deseeded and chopped

1. Heat the oil in a wok or large frying pan until smoking. Add the chicken strips and stir-fry for 2 minutes to seal. Add the green beans, reduce the heat, cover and cook for a further 5 minutes, stirring halfway through to prevent burning, until the chicken is cooked through. Keep warm by covering with a lid.

2. Meanwhile, prepare the dressing. Mix the fish sauce, honey, lemon juice and chopped chilli together in a small bowl. Set aside. Toss the Chinese leaves and peanuts together with the chopped coriander in a large serving bowl.

3. Add the mango, warm chicken and green beans to the serving bowl, then pour over the dressing. Toss to coat and serve immediately.

cals: 436   fat: 18.5g   sat fat: 3g   fibre: 6.2g   carbs: 31g   sugar: 21.2g   salt: 2.4g   protein: 40.5g

dairy-free alternatives

Many people with allergies or intolerances like to make their food from scratch as they prefer to eat natural foods that are fresh and not treated with flavour enhancers or preservatives. There are many good, natural alternatives to dairy nowadays for use in all types of recipes.

no dairy

Replacements for butter

Many people prefer to use margarine instead of butter in cooking and making this switch seems straightforward. It is important to realize that not all margarines are suitable for people with dairy allergies or intolerances – many still contain dairy products so you will need to carefully check the labels. There are all sorts of dairy-free margarines and butter substitutes available and new products are being developed all the time. Products vary, but margarines may contain more water than fat and this can have adverse effects when it is used for certain recipes, such as in cakes or breads. Some people who are conscious of their health are also concerned that margarine is not a 'natural' product and often contains unhealthy trans fats. For these reasons, it is a good idea to also use light vegetable oil, such as rapeseed or coconut oil.

Replacements for milk

Soya milk was the first dairy-free milk replacement to be widely commercially available, but the market is expanding rapidly. Most supermarkets and health stores now stock milks made from almonds, rice, oats, coconuts and hazelnuts, and these are becoming popular with the general population looking to eat less dairy as well. Dairy-free milks of all kinds tend to contain less fat and more water than dairy milk and this can affect results in certain recipes, especially when baking. Soya milk has a particular tendency to

curdle when vinegar or lemon juice is added and, although this looks rather unpleasant, the result is a useful substitute for buttermilk in dairy-free cooking.

Replacements for cream and yogurt

All kinds of dairy-free creams and yogurts are now being developed, many based on soya or coconut milk. These can work well but results can be unpredictable when they are used in cooking, with some products splitting and then becoming watery. Coconut cream is satisfyingly creamy but high in saturated fats, making it more suitable for occasional treats than everyday use.

Other dairy-free ingredients

People with dairy allergies or intolerances also need to take care with some other ingredients, too. Dark chocolate is not necessarily dairy free and, although there are good varieties of dairy-free chocolate available (including substitutes for milk and white chocolate), these may behave unpredictably when heated, separating into an oil mixture or hardening into lumps so work carefully and slowly with these ingredients. Dairy-free cream cheese is also available in health stores.

A dairy-free diet

As dairy produce is such a good source of protein, calcium and vitamins A and B12, then people excluding this from their diet should take care. A dairy-free diet should include green leafy vegetables, fortified soya products, canned fish like sardines which are eaten along with their bones, pulses and cereals. Anyone following a dairy-free diet should talk to their doctor about the possibility of taking calcium supplements.

seared beef salad

prep: 20-25 mins
cook: 6-10 mins, plus resting

½ iceberg lettuce, leaves separated and torn into bite-sized pieces

200 g/7 oz radishes, thinly sliced

4 shallots, thinly sliced

85 g/3 oz kale, shredded

2 tbsp dried goji berries

25 g/1 oz fresh mint, roughly chopped

25 g/1 oz fresh coriander, roughly chopped

2 x 250 g/9 oz sirloin steaks, visible fat removed

4 tbsp sunflower oil

juice of 1 lime

1 tbsp tamari

salt and pepper

fact

Fresh mint leaves freshen the palate and are thought to help relieve symptoms of irritable bowel syndrome by relieving bloating and abdominal discomfort.

1. Put the lettuce, radishes and shallots in a serving bowl. Sprinkle over the kale, goji berries, mint and coriander, then toss the salad gently together.

2. Preheat a ridged griddle pan over a high heat. Brush the steaks with 1 tablespoon of oil, then sprinkle with a little salt and pepper. Cook in the hot pan for 2 minutes on each side for medium-rare, 3 minutes for medium or 4 minutes for well done. Transfer the steaks to a plate and leave to rest for a few minutes.

3. Meanwhile, to make the dressing, put the lime juice, tamari and remaining 3 tablespoons of oil in a jam jar, screw on the lid and shake well. Drizzle over the salad, then toss together.

4. Divide the salad between four bowls. Thinly slice the steak and arrange it over the top, then serve immediately.

shaker salad in a jar

prep: 20 mins
cook: no cooking

2 crisp red eating apples
lime juice, for sprinkling
1 large carrot
6-cm/2½-inch piece cucumber
85 g/3 oz mung bean sprouts
55 g/2 oz sunflower seed sprouts
40 g/1½ oz alfalfa seed sprouts

dressing
1 tbsp lime juice
3 tbsp olive oil
1 tsp grated fresh ginger
1 tsp light muscovado sugar
salt and pepper, to taste

1. Quarter, core and roughly grate the apples into a bowl, then sprinkle with lime juice to prevent browning. Roughly grate the carrot and the cucumber into two separate bowls.

2. To make the dressing, place all of the dressing ingredients in a large jar or sealable food container, large enough to hold the salad with room to spare. Shake well to mix.

3. Add all the bean and seed sprouts to the jar, then layer the apple, carrot and cucumber into the jar. Replace the lid until required.

4. To serve, shake the jar to coat the ingredients in the dressing, then either eat straight from the jar or transfer to bowls.

top tip

To sprout the seeds, soak overnight in a jar of cold water, drain, then rinse and drain twice a day for 3–5 days until sprouted.

cals: 266   fat: 18.3g   sat fat: 2.4g   fibre: 5g   carbs: 23.4g   sugar: 13.6g   salt: 1.8g   protein: 4.8g

polenta bruschettas with tapenade

prep: 25 mins, plus setting
cook: 15-20 mins

500 ml/17 fl oz boiling water
100 g/3½ oz quick-cook polenta
2 tbsp olive oil, plus extra for greasing
16 cherry vine tomatoes
salt and pepper

tapenade
25 g/1 oz sun-dried tomatoes
55 g/2 oz pitted black olives
2 tbsp salted capers, rinsed
2 tbsp chopped fresh flat-leaf parsley
1 garlic clove, crushed
juice of ½ lemon
2 tbsp extra virgin olive oil

1. Place the water in a saucepan with a pinch of salt and bring to the boil. Sprinkle in the polenta and stir over a medium heat for about 5 minutes, or until thick and smooth.

2. Grease a 450 g/1 lb loaf tin. Stir the oil into the polenta mix and season to taste, then spread into the prepared tin. Leave to set.

3. To make the tapenade, finely chop the sun-dried tomatoes, olives, capers and parsley. Mix with the garlic, lemon juice and oil, and season to taste.

4. Preheat the grill to high. Cut the polenta into eight slices and arrange on a baking sheet with the tomatoes. Brush the polenta with oil and grill until golden, turning once.

5. Serve the polenta slices topped with a spoonful of tapenade and the tomatoes.

easy vegetable sushi

prep: 30–35 mins, plus cooling and chilling
cook: 25 mins

200 g/7 oz sushi rice

2–3 tbsp Japanese rice vinegar

pinch of salt

1 tbsp Japanese sweet rice wine (mirin)

7 sheets Japanese sushi nori, pretoasted

½ cucumber, cut into matchsticks

1 red pepper, deseeded and cut into matchsticks

1 avocado, cut into matchsticks

4 spring onions, halved lengthwise

tamari, gluten-free wasabi and sliced ginger, to serve (optional)

top tip

This vegetarian dish makes a great light lunch and although it is tricky to make, the tasty result is worth the effort The wasabi adds a spicy kick too!

1. Place the rice in a saucepan and cover with 375 ml/13 fl oz of water. Bring to the boil, then reduce the heat to low, cover and simmer for 20 minutes. Drain the rice and transfer to a large bowl. Gently fold in the rice vinegar, salt and mirin and leave to cool.

2. When the rice is cold, place one sheet of pretoasted nori onto a sushi rolling mat, shiny side down, and spread a thin layer of rice all over, leaving a 1-cm/½-inch border along the far edge. Add a selection of the vegetable pieces, arranged in lines running the same way as the bamboo of the mat.

3. Use the mat to carefully lift the edge of the nori closest to you, roll it away from you and tuck it in as tightly as you can. Continue to roll the nori up tightly and, if necessary, moisten the far edge with a little water to seal the roll together. Repeat with the remaining nori sheets, rice and vegetables. Chill the rolls in the refrigerator, wrapped tightly in clingfilm, until required.

4. To serve, cut each roll into slices about 2.5 cm/1 inch thick. Serve with tamari and wasabi for dipping and sliced ginger as an accompaniment, if desired.

cals: 278   fat: 5.9g   sat fat: 0.8g   fibre: 6.9g   carbs: 50.5g   sugar: 4.4g   salt: 0.8g   protein: 6.7g

monkfish ceviche with red quinoa

prep: 25 mins, plus marinating
cook: 20 mins, plus standing

450 g/1 lb monkfish fillets or other firm white fish, cubed

juice of 5–6 limes

60 g/2¼ oz red quinoa, rinsed

150 ml/5 fl oz water

4 tomatoes

1 red onion, diced

1–2 small fresh green jalapeño chillies, deseeded and diced

4 tbsp chopped fresh coriander

1 large, ripe avocado, peeled, stoned and cubed

extra virgin olive oil, for drizzling

salt and pepper

lime wedges, to garnish

fact

You can buy quinoa in red, white or black grains. It is botanically related to beetroot and spinach and trumps the nutrition content of all other grains.

1. Put the fish into a shallow, non-metallic dish. Pour over enough of the lime juice to cover and marinate in the refrigerator for 3 hours, stirring occasionally, until opaque. Drain the fish, discarding the juice.

2. Put the quinoa into a saucepan with the water. Bring to the boil, then reduce the heat, cover and simmer for 15 minutes. Remove from the heat, but leave the pan covered for a further 5 minutes to allow the grains to swell. Fluff up with a fork and set aside.

3. Halve the tomatoes and discard the seeds. Cut into small dice, and put into a bowl with the onion, chillies and coriander. Stir in the remaining lime juice. Season to taste.

4. Divide the tomato mixture between four plates. Top with the fish and 2 tablespoons of the quinoa. (Reserve the remainder for use in another dish.) Scatter over the avocado.

5. Sprinkle with salt and drizzle with oil. Garnish with lime wedges and serve immediately.

cals: 330 cals   fat: 17g   sat fat: 2.5g   fibre: 6.7g   carbs: 26.2g   sugar: 5.1g   salt: 1.6g   protein: 21.1g

chicken balls with dipping sauce

prep: 25-30 mins
cook: 18-26 mins

2 large skinless, boneless chicken breasts
3 tbsp vegetable oil
2 shallots, finely chopped
½ celery stick, finely chopped
1 garlic clove, crushed
2 tbsp tamari
1 small egg, lightly beaten
1 bunch of spring onions
salt and pepper

dipping sauce
3 tbsp tamari
1 tbsp rice wine
1 tsp sesame seeds

fact

Chicken is a dense source of protein and we also receive a good dose of iron from eating chicken as well. Free-range chickens have a higher ratio of protein to fat

1. Cut the chicken into 2-cm/¾-inch pieces. Heat half of the oil in a frying pan and stir-fry the chicken over a high heat for 2–3 minutes, until golden. Remove from the pan with a slotted spoon and set aside.

2. Add the shallots, celery and garlic and stir-fry for 1–2 minutes, until softened.

3. Place the chicken and vegetables in a food processor and process until finely minced. Add 1 tablespoon of tamari and enough egg to make a firm mixture. Season to taste.

4. To make the dipping sauce, mix together the tamari, rice wine and sesame seeds in a small serving bowl and set aside.

5. Shape the chicken mixture into 16 walnut-sized balls. Heat the remaining oil in the pan and stir-fry the balls in small batches for 4–5 minutes, until golden. Drain on kitchen paper.

6. Add the spring onions to the pan and stir-fry for 1–2 minutes, until they begin to soften, then stir in the remaining tamari. Serve the chicken balls with the stir-fried spring onions and the dipping sauce.

cals: 251   fat: 14.1g   sat fat: 2g   fibre: 1.4g   carbs: 5.1g   sugar: 1.8g   salt: 4.2g   protein: 25.8g

vietnamese tofu & noodle salad

prep: 30 mins, plus marinating and cooling
cook: 12 mins

400 g/14 oz firm chilled plain tofu, drained and cut into 8 slices

115 g/4 oz buckwheat soba noodles

200 g/7 oz frozen edamame beans

1 carrot, cut into matchstick strips

85 g/3 oz mangetout, cut into matchstick strips

115 g/4 oz rainbow chard, stems cut into strips, leaves thinly shredded

15 g/½ oz fresh coriander, chopped

marinade

2 tbsp tamari

2 tbsp sesame seeds

1 red chilli, deseeded and finely chopped (optional)

4-cm/1½-inch piece fresh ginger, peeled and finely chopped

dressing

4 tbsp rapeseed oil

juice of ½ lemon

1 tbsp gluten-free sweet chilli sauce

1. Line the base of the grill pan with foil. Arrange the tofu on the grill pan in a single layer and fold up the edges of the foil to make a dish.

2. To make the marinade, mix together the tamari, sesame seeds, chilli, if using, and half of the ginger in a small bowl. Spoon this over the tofu, then leave to marinate for 10 minutes.

3. Bring a large saucepan of water to the boil, add the noodles and frozen edamame beans and cook for 3-4 minutes, or until just tender. Drain into a sieve, then rinse under cold running water.

4. Put the carrot, mangetout, rainbow chard stems and leaves and coriander in a large salad bowl. Add the noodles and edamame beans and gently toss.

5. To make the dressing, put the oil, lemon juice, sweet chilli sauce and remaining ginger in a bowl and whisk with a fork. Pour over the salad and gently toss.

6. Preheat the grill to medium-high. Turn the tofu over in the marinade, then grill for 2 minutes on each side, or until browned. Leave to cool for a few minutes, then cut into cubes and sprinkle over the salad with any remaining marinade and serve.

serves 4

cals: 383   fat: 20.3g   sat fat: 1.8g   fibre: 3.9g   carbs: 33.2g   sugar: 5.9g   salt: 1.3g   protein: 18.9g

watch out!

Always read labels on commercially prepared foods, as a surprising number contain hidden wheat, gluten or dairy products or derivatives. Check ready meals, burgers, sausages, sauces, soups, stock cubes and some brands of baking powder. Oven chips may have a wheat coating.

spoilt for choice!

There are quite a few ingredients that are naturally gluten and dairy free and form good bases for dinners. These include rice, eggs, beans and pulses, quinoa, meat and poultry, fish and shellfish, fresh fruit and vegetables, nuts and seeds, rice noodles, soya and tofu. So there really is lots of choice!

innertime feasts

five-spice tuna steaks	82
mexican chicken with rice	84
creole turkey-stuffed peppers	86
sweet potato & lentil stew	88
beef fried rice	90
barbecue-glazed spare ribs	92
raw shoots & seeds super salad	94
chicken chilli	96
grilled salmon with mango & lime salsa	98
GET GLUTEN FREE!	100
chimichurri steak	102
jamaican rice & peas with tofu	104
spatchcocked chicken with lemon	106
pork meatballs in a chilli broth	108
ginger & miso stir-fry	110
thai fish curry	112
jambalaya	114
roast chicken	116

five-spice tuna steaks

prep: 20-25 mins
cook: 10-14 mins

600 g/1 lb 5 oz tuna steaks

1 tbsp toasted sesame oil

2 tbsp lime juice

2 tbsp Chinese five spice

4 tbsp groundnut oil

1 large garlic clove, sliced

1-cm/½-inch piece fresh ginger, sliced

1 shallot, chopped

4 tbsp gluten-free chicken stock

1 tsp tamari

200 g/7 oz pak choi, stems and leaves
    chopped separately

3 tbsp chopped fresh coriander

sea salt and pepper

1. Cut the fish into 3-cm/1¼-inch chunks. Place in a shallow dish and sprinkle with the sesame oil and half of the lime juice, turning to coat thoroughly. Add the Chinese five spice, making sure to rub the spice well into the fish. Sprinkle with salt and pepper.

2. Heat a large wok over a high heat. Add half the groundnut oil and heat until just smoking. Add the fish and stir-fry for 3–4 minutes. Transfer to a plate and keep warm. Wipe out the wok. Reduce the heat to medium–high, add the remaining oil, the garlic, ginger and shallot and stir-fry for 1 minute.

3. Stir in the stock and tamari, then add the pak choi stems. Stir-fry for 1 minute, add the pak choi leaves and stir-fry for 2 minutes until the stems are tender. Return the fish to the wok and stir-fry briefly. Stir in the remaining lime juice and coriander and season well before serving.

top tip

Use a wok with a long wooden
handle. Wood will stay cool despite
the intense heat of the wok.

mexican chicken with rice

prep: 25 mins
cook: 1¼ hours

6 skinless chicken thighs on the bone, about 800 g/1 lb 12 oz total weight

1 litre/1¾ pints water

400 g/14 oz canned chopped tomatoes

2 bay leaves

2 pickled serrano or jalapeño chillies, chopped

2 limes, sliced

1 onion, halved

1 tbsp Mexican oregano

2 tsp ancho chilli powder

2 tsp ground coriander

2 tsp ground cumin

300 g/10½ oz easy-cook long-grain rice

salt and pepper

to serve (optional)

chopped fresh coriander

2 avocados, peeled, stoned, diced and tossed with lime juice

other accompaniments of your choice, such as pitted black olives, plain soya yogurt, chopped cherry tomatoes and chopped jalapeño peppers

1. Put the chicken and water into a saucepan and slowly bring to the boil, skimming the surface as necessary. When the foam stops rising, stir in the tomatoes, bay leaves, chillies, lime slices, onion, oregano, chilli powder, ground coriander and cumin and season to taste with salt and pepper. Adjust the heat so the liquid just bubbles, then leave to bubble for about 1 hour until the liquid evaporates and the meat is very tender. The juices should run clear when a skewer is inserted into the thickest part of the meat.

2. Meanwhile, cook the rice according to the packet instructions, then drain well and keep hot.

3. Use a slotted spoon to transfer the chicken mixture to a bowl. Remove the bones and use two forks to shred the meat. Adjust the seasoning, if necessary.

4. To serve, divide the rice between four warmed bowls, then top with the shredded chicken. Sprinkle with chopped coriander and serve with the remaining accompaniments in small bowls for adding at the table.

serves 4

cals: 642   fat: 17.8g   sat fat: 4.5g   fibre: 5.6g   carbs: 77g   sugar: 7.3g   salt: 2g   protein: 44.9g

creole turkey-stuffed peppers

prep: 25 mins
cook: 50-55 mins

4 large red peppers,
   about 200 g/7 oz each

1 tbsp sunflower oil,
   plus extra for greasing

40 g/1½ oz gluten-free chorizo,
   skinned and diced

300 g/10½ oz fresh turkey mince

1 celery stick, finely chopped

1 onion, finely chopped

1 small green pepper, deseeded and
   finely chopped

100 g/3½ oz long-grain easy-cook rice

200 ml/7 fl oz gluten-free vegetable
   stock

4 tbsp passata

2 tbsp chopped fresh parsley or
   snipped chives

½ tsp gluten-free hot pepper sauce,
   plus extra to serve

salt and pepper

salad leaves, to serve (optional)

1. Preheat the oven to 220°C/425°F/Gas Mark 7 and grease a baking dish. Cut off the red pepper tops and remove the cores and seeds, then set the peppers and tops aside.

2. Heat the oil in a frying pan over a medium heat. Add the chorizo and fry for 1–2 minutes until it gives off its oil. Transfer to a dish using a slotted spoon and set aside.

3. Pour off all but 2 tablespoons of oil from the pan. Add the turkey, celery, onion and green pepper and fry, stirring with a wooden spoon to break up the turkey into large clumps, for 3–5 minutes until the onion is soft. Stir in the rice.

4. Add the stock, passata, parsley, hot pepper sauce, and salt and pepper to taste. Bring to the boil, stirring. Divide the mixture between the red peppers, then arrange them in the prepared dish, topped with their 'lids'. Carefully pour in boiling water to fill the dish up to 2.5 cm/1 inch, then cover tightly with foil.

5. Bake in the preheated oven for 40–45 minutes, or until the peppers are tender. Serve hot or at room temperature, with salad leaves and the chorizo.

cals: 382   fat: 17.7g   sat fat: 4.6g   fibre: 5.2g   carbs: 36.4g   sugar: 10g   salt: 2.4g   protein: 19.4g

sweet potato & lentil stew

prep: 15–20 mins
cook: 30 mins

2 tbsp olive oil

350 g/12 oz sweet potato,
   cut into 1-cm/½-inch cubes

1 onion, chopped

1 carrot, chopped

1 leek, sliced

1 bay leaf

85 g/3 oz Puy lentils

750 ml/1¼ pints gluten-free stock

1 tbsp chopped fresh sage

salt and pepper

1. Heat the oil in a large saucepan or stockpot over a low heat. Gently fry the sweet potato, onion, carrot, leek and bay leaf for 5 minutes.

2. Stir in the lentils, stock and sage, and bring to the boil. Reduce the heat and simmer for 20 minutes, or until the lentils are tender but not disintegrating.

3. Season to taste with salt and pepper, then remove and discard the bay leaf. Serve immediately.

serves 4

cals: 261   fat: 8.3g   sat fat: 1.7g   fibre: 11.2g   carbs: 41g   sugar: 8.1g   salt: 2.6g   protein: 8.1g

beef fried rice

prep: 15 mins
cook: 30-35 mins

500 g/1 lb 2 oz long-grain rice

2 tbsp groundnut oil

4 large eggs, lightly beaten

650 g/1 lb 7 oz fresh beef mince

1 large onion, finely chopped

2 garlic cloves, finely chopped

140 g/5 oz frozen peas

3 tbsp tamari

1 tsp sugar

salt

gluten-free prawn crackers, to serve
  (optional)

1. Cook the rice in a large saucepan of salted boiling water for 15 minutes, until tender. Drain and rinse with boiling water. Set aside.

2. Heat a wok over a medium heat, then add the groundnut oil, swirl it around the wok and heat. Add the eggs and cook, stirring constantly, for 50–60 seconds, until set. Transfer to a dish and set aside.

3. Add the beef and stir-fry, breaking it up with a wooden spoon, for 4–5 minutes, until evenly browned. Stir in the onion, garlic and peas and stir-fry for a further 3–4 minutes.

4. Add the rice, tamari, sugar and eggs and cook, stirring constantly, for a further 1–2 minutes, until heated through. Serve immediately with prawn crackers.

top tip

This dish is perfect for using up left-over rice. You can also use any meat and vegetables, making it the ideal storecupboard supper.

cals: 671   fat: 25g   sat fat: 8.4g   fibre: 2.8g   carbs: 74.8g   sugar: 3.7g   salt: 2.1g   protein: 33.3g

barbecue-glazed
spare ribs

prep: 20 mins
cook: 1¼ hours

2 racks pork spare ribs,
   about 800 g/1 lb 12 oz each

3 tbsp instant coffee granules, dissolved
   in 6 tbsp hot water

6 tbsp gluten-free tomato ketchup

2 tbsp vegetable oil

3 tbsp gluten-free Worcestershire sauce

3 tbsp gluten-free mango chutney

salt and pepper

salad, to serve (optional)

fact

Pork is a good source of protein and
contains many other key nutrients — for
example, it is very high in potassium,
zinc and iron.

1. Put the racks of ribs into a large saucepan and cover with water. Bring to the boil, skim off any scum from the surface, then simmer for 25 minutes.

2. Lift the ribs out of the water and place on a metal rack set over a large roasting tin. Preheat the oven to 190°C/375°F/ Gas Mark 5.

3. Put the coffee, tomato ketchup, oil, Worcestershire sauce and chutney into a bowl and mix together. Season to taste with salt and pepper.

4. Liberally brush the coffee glaze over the racks of ribs. Roast in the preheated oven for 45 minutes, basting occasionally, until the glaze is sticky and lightly charred in places and the ribs are tender.

5. Serve the glazed ribs immediately with salad on the side.

cals: 910   fat: 66.8g   sat fat: 30.9g   fibre: 0.4g   carbs: 17.3g   sugar: 12.8g   salt: 3.2g   protein: 66.6g

raw shoots & seeds super salad

prep: 20 mins
cook: no cooking

225 g/8 oz mixed sprouted seeds and
beans (such as alfalfa, mung beans,
soy beans, aduki beans, chickpeas
and radish seeds)

30 g/1 oz pumpkin seeds

30 g/1 oz sunflower seeds

30 g/1 oz sesame seeds

1 small apple

70 g/2½ oz ready-to-eat dried apricots

grated rind and juice of 1 lemon

50 g/1¾ oz walnuts, roughly chopped

2 tbsp olive oil

1. In a large mixing bowl, combine the sprouts
and seeds. Core and chop the apple and chop
the apricots into small pieces. Stir the fruit
into the bowl, then stir in the lemon rind
and walnuts.

2. Make a dressing by mixing the lemon juice
with the oil in a small bowl using a fork to
thoroughly combine.

3. Stir the lemon dressing into the salad and
serve immediately.

fact

This is an incredibly healthy,
low-fat dinner, packed with seeds,
fruits, nuts and beans.

chicken chilli

prep: 20-25 mins
cook: 40 mins

1 tbsp vegetable oil

1 onion, diced

2 garlic cloves, finely chopped

1 green pepper, deseeded and diced

1 small jalapeño pepper, deseeded and diced

2 tsp gluten-free chilli powder

2 tsp dried oregano

1 tsp ground cumin

1 tsp salt

500 g/1 lb 2 oz canned cannellini beans, drained and rinsed

750 ml/1¼ pints gluten-free chicken stock

450 g/1 lb cooked chicken breasts, shredded

juice of 1 lime

25 g/1 oz chopped fresh coriander

1. Heat the oil in a large, heavy-based saucepan over a medium–high heat. Add the onion, garlic, pepper and jalapeño and cook, stirring occasionally, for about 5 minutes or until soft. Add the chilli powder, oregano, cumin and salt and cook, stirring, for about a further 30 seconds.

2. Add the beans and stock and bring to the boil. Reduce the heat to medium–low and simmer gently, uncovered, for about 20 minutes.

3. Ladle about half of the bean mixture into a blender or food processor and purée. Return the purée to the pan along with the shredded chicken. Simmer for about 10 minutes or until heated through. Just before serving, stir in the lime juice and coriander. Serve immediately.

cals: 243   fat: 6.3g   sat fat: 1.6g   fibre: 6.5g   carbs: 16.3g   sugar: 2.8g   salt: 2.2g   protein: 30.1g

grilled salmon with mango & lime salsa

prep: 20 mins
cook: 8–10 mins

2 tbsp lime juice
1 tbsp clear honey
1 tbsp chopped fresh dill
4 salmon fillets, about 115 g/4 oz each
salt and pepper
boiled new potatoes and salad leaves,
   to serve (optional)

salsa
1 ripe mango, peeled, stoned and diced
finely grated rind and juice of 1 lime
2 tbsp desiccated coconut
1 tbsp chopped fresh dill

1. Preheat a grill to high and lay a piece of foil on a grill pan. Mix together the lime juice, honey and dill in a wide dish. Season to taste with salt and pepper.

2. Place the salmon fillets in the dish and turn to coat evenly in the glaze. Arrange on the prepared grill pan and grill for 4–5 minutes on each side, turning once, or until cooked through.

3. Meanwhile, prepare the salsa. Mix the mango in a small bowl with the lime rind and juice. Stir in the coconut and dill.

4. Serve the salmon hot, with the salsa spooned over the top and new potatoes and salad leaves alongside, if desired.

top tip

Prick a fresh lime and microwave it on high for 30 seconds to get much more juice from it

cals: 334   fat: 17.7g   sat fat: 5.3g   fibre: 2.5g   carbs: 20.4g   sugar: 16.5g   salt: 1.7g   protein: 24.6g

get gluten free!

Most supermarkets and health food shops stock a useful range of gluten-free alternatives for restricted diets. Free-from substitutes are a useful dietary addition for those excluding a food group. However, there are also lots of ingredients that are naturally gluten free so there really is a whole range to choose from.

free from

Gluten-free ingredients

Coeliacs and those with gluten sensitivity can eat other types of grains, including all forms of rice, buckwheat, amaranth, millet, quinoa, tapioca, sago, corn and maize. Some coeliacs may be able to tolerate moderate amounts of oats, but they must be from an uncontaminated source, to avoid contamination with other grains during processing. Gluten-free flour, made from blends of rice, potato, tapioca and buckwheat flours, is useful for baking. Some self-raising blends have xanthan gum added for elasticity, to improve texture in cakes. Single-grain flours like corn, rice or gram flour can be used for thickening sauces, binding or coating. Gluten-free pasta, breads and crackers are available in most supermarkets or health food shops.

Gluten-free labelling

Nowadays new labelling legislation has made it much easier for coeliacs when purchasing gluten-free products. Products may now only be labelled as gluten-free if the product has less than 20 parts per million of gluten. Companies that produce and package food in the UK must legally have an ingredients list. The manufacturer must therefore state if wheat, rye, oats and barley have been used in their product. Ingredients which have been made from cereals which contain gluten such as glucose syrup, maltodextrin and distilled ingredients are now processed to remove the gluten so are, therefore, gluten-free. Although allergy boxes are not a legal requirement, some manufacturers have begun to use them in recent years. If an allergy box is used on a product it is still necessary to check that it is suitable for your requirements. Today the Food Standards Agency provides guidance to manufacturers with regards to the term 'May Contain'. Manufacturers may use this term on their labelling if they feel that there is a risk that their product may have been contaminated by gluten. Only companies which specialize in producing gluten-free food products are able to use the term 'Gluten-free' or 'Suitable for Coeliacs' on their labelling. Other countries are also establishing new laws about the labelling of gluten-free products.

Gluten-free foods

The following foods are all gluten free:
- meat and poultry
- fish and shellfish
- beans and pulses
- fresh vegetables and fruit
- eggs
- corn and cornmeal (maize/sweetcorn)
- fats, such as oil
- rice and wild rice
- rice noodles
- soya and plain tofu
- nuts and seeds
- sugar and honey
- treacle, golden syrup and maple syrup
- vanilla extract
- fresh herbs and spices
- fresh and dried yeast
- spirits (including whisky and malt whisky)
- wines and sparkling wines
- port, sherry and liqueurs
- cider

chimichurri steak

prep: 25 mins
cook: 15 mins, plus resting

675–900 g/1 lb 8 oz–2 lb sirloin steak

4 fresh corn cobs

1 shallot

3 garlic cloves

4 tbsp gluten-free sherry vinegar

60 g/2¼ oz fresh flat-leaf parsley, chopped

1 tbsp fresh oregano leaves, chopped

½ tsp crushed red pepper flakes

125 ml/4 fl oz olive oil

juice of 1 lemon

salt and pepper

1. Preheat the grill to medium–high. Generously season the steak with salt and pepper. Remove the corn husks and silks, season the cobs and wrap individually in foil.

2. To make the sauce, finely chop the shallot and garlic and place them in a small bowl with the vinegar and 1 teaspoon of salt. Add the parsley and oregano to the vinegar mixture along with the red pepper flakes. Whisk in the oil until well combined. Stir in the lemon juice. Put the corn and the steak on the grill rack. Cook the steak, turning once, for about 4 minutes per side for medium-rare, until nicely seared on the outside. Turn the corn occasionally, cooking it for 15 minutes in total.

3. Transfer the meat to a chopping board and leave to rest for 4 minutes. Slice it against the grain into 5-mm/¼-inch thick slices. Serve the meat drizzled with the sauce and with the corn on the side.

variation

Substitute the sauce with a
gluten and dairy-free pesto sauce,
thinned with a bit of lemon juice
and olive oil.

jamaican rice & peas with tofu

prep: 20 mins
cook: 25-30 mins

250 g/9 oz firm plain tofu, cubed

2 tbsp chopped fresh thyme,
   plus extra sprigs to garnish

2 tbsp olive oil

1 onion, sliced

1 garlic clove, crushed

1 small fresh red chilli, chopped

400 ml/14 fl oz gluten-free stock

200 g/7 oz basmati rice

4 tbsp coconut cream

400 g/14 oz canned red kidney
   beans, drained and rinsed

salt and pepper

1. Toss the tofu with half the chopped thyme and sprinkle with salt and pepper to taste.

2. Heat 1 tablespoon of the oil in a large pan, add the tofu and fry, stirring occasionally, for 2 minutes. Remove and keep warm.

3. Add the remaining oil to the pan, then add the onion and fry, stirring, for 3–4 minutes. Stir in the garlic, chilli and the remaining chopped thyme, then add the stock and bring to the boil. Stir in the rice, then reduce the heat, cover and simmer for 12–15 minutes, until the rice is tender.

4. Stir in the coconut cream and beans, season to taste with salt and pepper and cook gently for 2–3 minutes. Spoon the tofu over the rice and serve hot, garnished with thyme sprigs.

top tip

Cut the tofu cubes into equal sizes
to ensure they cook evenly.

cals: 478   fat: 19.8g   sat fat: 9.8g   fibre: 6.7g   carbs: 59g   sugar: 3g   salt: 2.5g   protein: 14.1g

spatchcocked chicken with lemon

prep: 25–30 mins, plus standing
cook: 45–55 mins, plus resting

2 tbsp clear honey

1 tbsp freshly squeezed lemon juice

¼ tsp hot or sweet paprika, to taste

1 chicken, about 1.5 kg/3 lb 5 oz, spatchcocked

sunflower oil, for oiling

salt and pepper

finely chopped fresh flat-leaf parsley and grated lemon rind, to garnish

top tip

It is important to check that the chicken has been cooked thoroughly by inserting a skewer into the thickest part of the meat and checking the juices run clear.

1. Mix together the honey, lemon juice, paprika, and salt and pepper to taste in a wide, non-metallic bowl, large enough to hold the chicken flat.

2. Add the chicken and rub in the mixture all over, then leave to stand for 30 minutes at room temperature.

3. Meanwhile, preheat the oven to 190°C/375°F/Gas Mark 5. Put a greased rack into a roasting tin large enough to hold the chicken flat.

4. When ready to cook, oil two long metal skewers. Place the chicken on a chopping board and run the skewers through the body in an 'X' shape.

5. Place the chicken on the prepared rack, skin-side up, and brush with the marinade. Roast in the preheated oven for 45–55 minutes, brushing with the marinade twice, until the skin is golden brown and the juices run clear when the thickest part of the meat is pierced with a skewer.

6. Remove from the oven, cover with foil and leave to rest for 5 minutes. Use a metal spoon to skim the fat off the pan juices. Carve the chicken, spoon over the pan juices and garnish with the parsley and lemon rind.

pork meatballs in a chilli broth

prep: 30 mins, plus cooling and chilling
cook: 30 mins

1.2 litres/2 pints gluten-free chicken stock

¼–½ fresh red chilli, deseeded and very finely sliced

½ tsp palm sugar or soft light brown sugar

3 fresh thyme sprigs

2 lemon grass stalks, fibrous outer leaves removed, stems bashed with the flat of a knife

¼ tsp pepper

1 small head pak choi, stems cut into small squares, leaves sliced into ribbons

1 spring onion, sliced diagonally

dash of tamari

salt

pork meatballs

225 g/8 oz fresh pork mince

1 shallot, grated

2-cm/¾-inch piece fresh ginger, crushed

1 garlic clove, crushed

zest and juice of ½ lime, plus wedges to serve

6 tbsp groundnut oil

1. Pour the stock into a medium-sized saucepan. Add the chilli, sugar, thyme, lemon grass, pepper, and salt to taste and bring to the boil. Reduce the heat and simmer gently for 10 minutes. Remove from the heat and leave to cool for about 30 minutes.

2. To make the meatballs, combine the pork, shallot, ginger, garlic, lime zest and juice and season. Mix well with a fork. Line a plate with kitchen paper.

3. Divide the mixture into 16–20 walnut-sized balls. Place on the prepared plate and chill for 30 minutes.

4. Heat a large wok over a high heat. Add the oil and heat until very hot. Add the pork meatballs and fry for 5–6 minutes, until golden brown all over and cooked through. Drain on kitchen paper and keep warm.

5. Remove the thyme and lemon grass from the broth. Add the pak choi and spring onion. Bring to the boil then simmer for 2 minutes until the pak choi stalks are just tender. Season with tamari.

6. Ladle the broth and vegetables over the meatballs in bowls and serve immediately, with lime wedges on the side.

cals: 363   fat: 33.9g   sat fat: 8.7g   fibre: 1.1g   carbs: 6g   sugar: 2.1g   salt: 3g   protein: 11.1g

ginger & miso stir-fry

prep: 20 mins
cook: 8 mins

2 tbsp vegetable oil

1 tbsp sesame oil

1 green pepper, deseeded and
cut into matchsticks

1 red pepper, deseeded and
cut into matchsticks

¼ white cabbage, cored and
thinly sliced

1 carrot, cut into matchsticks

1 red chilli, deseeded and
finely chopped

6 spring onions, finely chopped

50 g/1¾ oz green soya
(edamame) beans

50 g/1¾ oz cashew nuts,
roughly chopped

freshly cooked rice, to serve (optional)

sauce

1 tsp gluten-free miso paste dissolved
in 2 tbsp boiling water

1 tbsp tomato purée

2.5-cm/1-inch piece fresh ginger,
peeled

fact

Soya beans are one of the few plant sources of complete protein. They are used here in the stir fry and in the miso paste, which is a tasty and savoury source of flavouring.

1. To make the sauce, mix together the warm miso and the tomato purée in a small bowl. Grate the ginger coarsely, then gather up the grated ginger and squeeze the juice into the miso mixture.

2. Heat the vegetable oil and sesame oil together in a large wok over a high heat. Stir-fry the peppers, cabbage, carrot, chilli, onions, soya beans and nuts for 5 minutes.

3. Stir in the miso-ginger sauce and cook for a further minute.

4. Serve immediately with rice.

cals: 457   fat: 33.8g   sat fat: 4.6g   fibre: 9.3g   carbs: 31.2g   sugar: 10.2g   salt: 0.4g   protein: 11.9g

thai fish curry

prep: 15 mins
cook: 15–20 mins

1 tbsp groundnut oil

2 spring onions, sliced

1 tsp cumin seeds, ground

2 fresh green chillies, chopped

1 tsp coriander seeds, ground

4 tbsp chopped fresh coriander

1 tsp chopped fresh mint, plus
   extra to garnish

1 tbsp snipped fresh chives

150 ml/5 fl oz light coconut milk

4 white fish fillets,
   about 225 g/8 oz each

salt and pepper

freshly cooked rice, to serve (optional)

1. Heat the oil in a large frying pan or shallow saucepan and add the spring onions. Fry the spring onions over a medium heat until they are softened but not coloured.

2. Stir in the cumin, chillies and ground coriander, and cook until fragrant. Add the fresh coriander, mint, chives and coconut milk and season to taste with salt and pepper.

3. Carefully place the fish fillets in the pan and poach for 10–15 minutes, or until the flesh flakes when tested with a fork.

4. Garnish the curry with the chopped mint and serve immediately, with the basmati rice on the side.

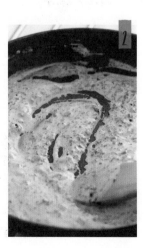
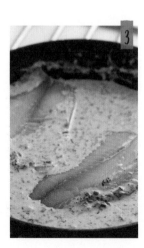

top tip

Groundnut oil, with its good balance of healthy fats, is the ideal oil to use in this recipe.

cals: 272   fat: 8.9g   sat fat: 4.3g   fibre: 1.3g   carbs: 4.6g   sugar: 1.9g   salt: 1.8g   protein: 41.5g

jambalaya

prep: 25 mins
cook: 35–45 mins

2 tbsp vegetable oil

2 onions, roughly chopped

1 green pepper, deseeded and
  roughly chopped

2 celery sticks, roughly chopped

3 garlic cloves, finely chopped

2 tsp paprika

300 g/10½ oz skinless, boneless
  chicken breasts, chopped

100 g/3½ oz gluten-free sausages,
  chopped

3 tomatoes, peeled and chopped

450 g/1 lb long-grain rice

900 ml/1½ pints gluten-free chicken
  stock or fish stock

1 tsp dried oregano

2 bay leaves

12 large raw prawns,
  peeled and deveined

4 spring onions, finely chopped

salt and pepper

chopped fresh flat-leaf parsley,
  to garnish

1. Heat the oil in a large frying pan over a low heat. Add the onions, green pepper, celery and garlic and cook for 8–10 minutes, until all the vegetables have softened.

2. Stir in the paprika and cook for a further 30 seconds. Add the chicken and sausages and cook for 8–10 minutes, or until lightly browned. Add the tomatoes and cook for 2–3 minutes, or until they have collapsed.

3. Add the rice to the pan and stir well. Pour in the stock, oregano and bay leaves and stir well. Cover and simmer for 10 minutes.

4. Add the prawns and stir. Re-cover and cook for a further 6–8 minutes, or until the rice is tender and the chicken and prawns are cooked through.

5. Stir in the spring onions and season to taste with salt and pepper. Remove and discard the bay leaves, garnish with parsley and serve immediately.

cals: 755   fat: 16g   sat fat: 3.8g   fibre: 5.6g   carbs: 108g   sugar: 7.3g   salt: 4.9g   protein: 43.2g

roast chicken

prep: 25-30 mins
cook: 25-30 mins

2 tbsp olive oil, plus extra if needed

1 small onion, chopped

450 g/1 lb Brussels sprouts, quartered

450 g/1 lb small, red-skinned new potatoes, quartered

12 baby carrots, peeled but left whole

1 fennel bulb, sliced into small wedges

4 skinned chicken legs (thighs and drumsticks)

4 tbsp gluten-free mustard

4 tbsp clear honey

1 tbsp gluten-free white wine vinegar

2 tsp garlic purée

¼–½ tsp cayenne pepper

50 ml/2 fl oz gluten-free chicken stock

1 tbsp fresh oregano leaves

50 ml/2 fl oz dry white wine

salt and pepper

top tip

To add extra flavour to this dish, make the mustard sauce the day before and then leave the chicken to marinate in this sauce overnight.

1. Preheat the oven to 240°C/475°F/Gas Mark 9. Heat the oil in a large, ovenproof frying pan. Add the onion, sprouts, potatoes, carrots and fennel.

2. Season the chicken with salt and pepper. Push the vegetables to the side of the pan. If necessary, add a little more oil to the pan. Add the chicken to the pan and cook for 2–3 minutes until brown on one side, then turn.

3. Meanwhile, combine the mustard, honey, vinegar, garlic purée, 1 teaspoon of salt, the cayenne pepper and stock in a bowl. Spoon the mixture over the turned chicken pieces to coat well. Drizzle the remaining sauce over the vegetables. Scatter the oregano over the chicken and vegetables.

4. Transfer the pan to the preheated oven and cook for about 20 minutes, or until the vegetables are tender and the chicken is cooked through (the juices should run clear when the thickest part of the meat is pierced with a skewer). Remove the pan from the oven and pour in the wine, stirring the vegetables and deglazing the pan. Serve immediately.

cals: 471   fat: 13.1g   sat fat: 2.3g   fibre: 10.1g   carbs: 56.6g   sugar: 24.2g   salt: 2.5g   protein: 34.2g

get baking!

Gluten and dairy-free baking can be tricky, but once you know which ingredients to work with and a few techniques then you'll be baking gorgeous loaves in no time! Some suitable gluten-free flours include amaranth, brown rice, buckwheat, chia, gram, millet, polenta, potato, sorghum and soya.

super sides & breads

vegetable pakoras — 120

spicy pak choi with sesame sauce — 122

roasted vegetables — 124

spring rolls — 126

hot & sour courgettes — 128

spiced basmati rice — 130

seven grain bread — 132

italian chickpea bread — 134

coriander flatbreads — 136

HOW TO BAKE GLUTEN FREE — 138

tomato focaccia — 140

courgette & polenta bread squares — 142

mixed grain bread — 144

mexican-style tortilla wraps — 146

herby scones — 148

quinoa & chive rolls — 150

fruit soda bread — 152

vegetable pakoras

prep: 25-30 mins
cook: 20-25 mins

6 tbsp gram flour

½ tsp salt

1 tsp gluten-free chilli powder

1 tsp gluten-free baking powder

1½ tsp white cumin seeds

1 tsp pomegranate seeds

300 ml/10 fl oz water

¼ bunch of fresh coriander, finely chopped, plus extra sprigs to garnish

vegetables of your choice, such as: cauliflower, cut into small florets; onions, cut into rings; potatoes, sliced; aubergines, sliced; or fresh spinach leaves

vegetable oil, for deep-frying

top tip

As the pakoras cook, transfer them to a wire rack placed on a baking tray in a low oven to keep warm until all the batches are cooked.

1. Sift the gram flour into a large bowl. Add the salt, chilli powder, baking powder, cumin and pomegranate seeds and stir together until well combined.

2. Pour in the water and beat well to form a smooth batter. Add the chopped coriander and mix well, then set aside.

3. Dip the prepared vegetables into the batter, carefully shaking off any excess.

4. Heat enough oil for deep-frying in a wok, deep-fat fryer or a large, heavy-based saucepan until it reaches 180°C/350°F, or until a cube of bread browns in 30 seconds. Using tongs, place the battered vegetables in the oil and deep-fry, in batches, turning once.

5. Repeat this process until all of the batter has been used up. Transfer the battered vegetables to crumpled kitchen paper and drain thoroughly. Garnish with coriander sprigs and serve immediately.

spicy pak choi with sesame sauce

prep: 15 mins, plus cooling
cook: 8-10 mins

2 tsp groundnut or vegetable oil
1 red chilli, deseeded and thinly sliced
1 garlic clove, thinly sliced
5 small pak choi, quartered
100 ml/3½ fl oz gluten-free stock

sauce
25 g/1 oz sesame seeds
2 tbsp tamari
2 tsp soft light brown sugar
1 garlic clove, crushed
3 tbsp sesame oil

1. For the sesame sauce, toast the sesame seeds in a dry frying pan set over a medium heat, stirring until lightly browned. Remove from the heat and cool slightly. Transfer to a pestle and mortar. Add the tamari, sugar and crushed garlic and pound to a coarse paste. Stir in the sesame oil.

2. Heat the groundnut oil in a wok or large frying pan. Add the chilli and sliced garlic and stir-fry for 20–30 seconds. Add the pak choi and stir-fry for 5 minutes, adding the stock a little at a time to prevent sticking.

3. Transfer the pak choi to a warmed dish, drizzle the sesame sauce over the top and serve immediately.

serves 4

variation

This pak choi tastes great when served with grilled salmon or stir-fried beef strips.

cals: 195   fat: 16g   sat fat: 2.3g   fibre: 2.5g   carbs: 8.7g   sugar: 4.5g   salt: 1.8g   protein: 4.6g

roasted vegetables

prep: 20–25 mins
cook: 35–40 mins

1 onion, cut into wedges

2–4 garlic cloves, left whole

1 aubergine, about 225 g/8 oz, trimmed and cut into cubes

2 courgettes, about 175 g/6 oz, trimmed and cut into chunks

300 g/10½ oz butternut squash, peeled, deseeded and cut into small wedges

2 assorted coloured peppers, deseeded and cut into chunks

2 tsp olive oil

1 tbsp shredded fresh basil

pepper

1. Preheat the oven to 200°C/400°F/Gas Mark 6. Place the onion wedges, whole garlic cloves and aubergine cubes in a large roasting tin.

2. Add the courgettes, squash and peppers to the roasting tin then pour over the oil. Turn the vegetables until they are lightly coated in the oil.

3. Roast the vegetables for 35–40 minutes, or until softened but not mushy. Turn the vegetables over occasionally during cooking.

4. Remove the vegetables from the oven, season with pepper to taste and stir. Scatter with shredded basil and serve immediately.

top tip

Try to ensure a wide mixture of colours for the vegetables to get a good range of nutrients.

cals: 114   fat: 2.8g   sat fat: 0.4g   fibre: 6g   carbs: 22g   sugar: 8.3g   salt: trace   protein: 3g

spring rolls

prep: 30 mins, plus marinating
cook: 15–20 mins

2 tbsp tamari

1½ tsp maple syrup

500 g/1 lb 2 oz lean pork fillets

vegetable oil, for frying

32 rice paper pancakes

75 ml/2½ fl oz gluten-free hoisin sauce, plus extra to serve

70 g/2½ oz rice vermicelli noodles, cooked

strips of cucumber and strips of spring onion, to serve

1. Blend the tamari and maple syrup in a dish. Add the pork and turn to coat. Cover and refrigerate for at least 1 hour.

2. Heat a griddle pan over a medium–high heat until hot, add a little oil to cover the base and cook the pork for 4–6 minutes each side, depending on the thickness of the fillets, until caramelized on the outside. Remove from the pan and slice into fine strips.

3. Fill a bowl with boiling water. Put 2 paper pancakes on top of one another (use 2 per roll) and soak in the water for 20 seconds, until pliable. Remove with a spatula, drain and place on a plate.

4. Spread a teaspoonful of hoisin sauce over the pancake and top with some noodles and strips of pork, cucumber and spring onion. Fold in the ends and sides of the pancake to resemble a spring roll. Make the rest of the rolls, then serve with any remaining sauce.

fact

Spring onions are rich sources of the cleansing mineral sulphur and help keep toxins at bay. They also contain more vitamin K than normal onions.

cals: 145   fat: 1.4g   sat fat: 0.3g   fibre: 0.4g   carbs: 24g   sugar: 2g   salt: 0.7g   protein: 8.3g

hot & sour courgettes

prep: 15-20 mins, plus standing
cook: 5 mins

2 large courgettes, thinly sliced

1 tsp salt

2 tbsp groundnut oil

1 tsp Sichuan peppercorns, crushed

½–1 red chilli, deseeded and sliced into thin strips

1 large garlic clove, thinly sliced

½ tsp finely chopped fresh ginger

1 tbsp rice vinegar

1 tbsp tamari

2 tsp sugar

1 spring onion, green part included, thinly sliced

a few drops of sesame oil and 1 tsp sesame seeds, to garnish

1. Put the courgette slices in a large colander and toss with the salt. Cover with a plate and put a weight on top. Leave to drain for 20 minutes. Rinse off the salt and spread out the slices on kitchen paper to dry.

2. Preheat a wok over a high heat and add the groundnut oil. Add the Sichuan peppercorns, chilli, garlic and ginger. Fry for about 20 seconds until the garlic is just beginning to colour.

3. Add the courgette slices and toss in the oil. Add the rice vinegar, tamari and sugar, and stir-fry for 2 minutes. Add the spring onion and fry for 30 seconds. Garnish with the sesame oil and seeds, and serve immediately.

serves 4

top tip

Don't miss out on salting as this draws out excess water that can make the dish soggy.

cals: 112   fat: 8.7g   sat fat: 1.4g   fibre: 1.6g   carbs: 7.7g   sugar: 5.6g   salt: 2.1g   protein: 2.3g

spiced basmati rice

prep: 10-15 mins, plus soaking
cook: 15-18 mins, plus standing

225 g/8 oz basmati rice
2 tbsp vegetable or groundnut oil
5 green cardamom pods, bruised
5 cloves
½ cinnamon stick
1 tsp fennel seeds
½ tsp black mustard seeds
2 bay leaves
450 ml/15 fl oz water
1½ tsp salt, or to taste
pepper

1. Rinse the rice in several changes of water until the water runs clear, then leave to soak for 30 minutes. Drain and set aside until ready to cook.

2. Heat a casserole or large saucepan with a tight-fitting lid over a medium–high heat, then add the oil. Add the spices and bay leaves and stir for 30 seconds. Stir the rice into the casserole so the grains are coated with oil. Stir in the water and salt and bring to the boil.

3. Reduce the heat to as low as possible and cover the casserole tightly. Simmer, without lifting the lid, for 8–10 minutes, or until the grains are tender and all the liquid has been absorbed.

4. Turn off the heat and use two forks to mix the rice. Season to taste with pepper. Re-cover the pan and leave to stand for 5 minutes before serving.

serves 4

top tip

Groundnut oil is higher in healthier types of fat than other oils, so use this if you can find it

cals: 270   fat: 7.3g   sat fat: 0.8g   fibre: 1.1g   carbs: 45.7g   sugar: 0.1g   salt: 2.2g   protein: 4.2g

seven grain bread

prep: 20-25 mins, plus rising and cooling
cook: 40-45 mins

oil, for greasing
60 g/2¼ oz amaranth flour
120 g/4¼ oz brown rice flour
120 g/4¼ oz sorghum flour
60 g/2¼ oz gluten-free cornflour
60 g/2¼ oz tapioca flour
20 g/¾ oz ground chia seeds
100 g/3½ oz ground linseeds
2 tsp xanthan gum
2 tsp easy-blend dried yeast
1 tsp salt
3 eggs
1 tbsp vegetable oil
2 tbsp sugar
240 ml/8½ fl oz tepid water
10 g/¼ oz sunflower seeds

fact

Sorghum is a lesser known flour and it has a nutty, sweet flavour. It is best used in conjunction with other flours, such as the amaranth, brown rice and tapioca flours here.

1. Grease a 450-g/1-lb loaf tin with oil.

2. Combine the flours, chia seeds, linseeds, xanthan gum, dried yeast and salt together in a bowl.

3. In a separate bowl, mix the eggs, vegetable oil, sugar and water together until well combined. Add the dry ingredients to the egg mixture and mix well to form a soft dough.

4. Put the dough into the prepared tin, sprinkle with the sunflower seeds and cover with a clean damp tea towel. Leave in a warm place for an hour until the dough rises. Preheat the oven to 180°C/350°F/Gas Mark 4.

5. Remove the tea towel and bake the loaf in the preheated oven for 40–45 minutes, or until golden brown. Remove from the oven and allow to cool in the tin. When cooled, remove from the tin.

cals: 3033   fat: 100.1g   sat fat: 29.8   fibre: 52g   carbs: 359.4g   sugar: 32.9g   salt: 7.5g   protein: 66.1g

italian chickpea bread

prep: 20 mins, plus standing and cooling
cook: 35-40 mins

250 g/9 oz gram (chickpea) flour
4 tbsp extra virgin olive oil
salt and pepper
sprigs of fresh rosemary, to garnish

1. Put the flour into a large mixing bowl. Gradually whisk in 900 ml/1½ pints of cold water using a balloon whisk or a hand-held electric whisk. Whisk the mixture until it is completely smooth and then stir in seasoning to taste. Set the bowl aside for 3 hours, to allow the batter to thicken.

2. Preheat the oven to 180°C/350°F/Gas Mark 4. Put the oil into a 33 x 23-cm/13 x 9-inch baking tray with a rim of at least 1 cm/½ inch.

3. Give the batter a quick stir with a wooden spoon and pour it into the baking tray, to form a layer that is approximately 5 mm/¼ inch thick. Arrange the rosemary sprigs in a decorative pattern on top of the batter.

4. Carefully put the baking tray into the preheated oven. A steady hand is useful as the oil underneath the wet batter tends to make it slide about in the tray.

5. Bake for 35–40 minutes, or until golden brown and firm. Allow to cool for 5 minutes in the tray before slicing.

top tip

This Italian-style bread, made with chickpea flour, is great for mopping up a rich tomato sauce.

cals: 117   fat: 5.2g   sat fat: 0.6g   fibre: 1.4g   carbs: 12g   sugar: trace   salt: 0.5g   protein: 4.9g

coriander flatbreads

prep: 20 mins
cook: 12 mins

200 g/7 oz buckwheat flour, plus extra
   for dusting
100 g/3½ oz rice flour
1 tsp salt
1 tsp gluten-free baking powder
½ tsp ground cumin
2 tbsp chopped fresh coriander
200 ml/7 fl oz water
2 tbsp olive oil

1. Sift the buckwheat flour, rice flour, salt, baking powder and cumin together into a large bowl and make a well in the centre.

2. Add the coriander, water and oil and stir into the dry ingredients to make a soft dough.

3. Divide the dough into four pieces and shape each piece into a smooth ball. Roll out each ball on a lightly floured surface to a 20-cm/8-inch round.

4. Preheat a griddle pan or barbecue to very hot. Add the flatbreads and cook for about 1 minute on each side, or until firm and golden brown. Serve warm.

2

fact

Despite its name, buckwheat flour does not contain wheat. It has a strong bitter flavour and is ideal for making flatbreads or pancakes.

how to bake gluten free

Finding gluten-free food is becoming easier all the time and substitutions are generally quite straightforward. However, baking without gluten can be tricky, especially if you are not using dairy. Many gluten-free baking recipes rely on the use of dairy to help bind mixtures and provide the elasticity that makes dough easier to work, and baked goods more likely to rise.

Anybody with a serious intolerance or allergy to gluten will be well aware of which baking ingredients are off-limits, but for other people, it might not be so obvious. Wheat, spelt, rye, barley and oats all contain gluten. Semolina and couscous also contain gluten as they are made with wheat. Some baking powder is not gluten free and you will need to make sure you check the label says gluten free. It's also important to realise that wheat free doesn't necessarily mean gluten free.

gluten-free flours and starches

Amaranth – best used as part of a gluten-free flour mix, this can improve the texture of a gluten-free bake and also adds to the nutritional value. It has a pleasant peppery flavour.

Arrowroot – a ground plant root that is used rather like cornflour as a thickener.

Brown and white rice flour – brown rice flour is heavier and more nutritious than white. Best used in combination with other gluten-free flours.

Buckwheat – this is not wheat and does not contain gluten. It has a strong, bitter flavour that works well in breads and pancakes.

Coconut flour – finely milled dried coconut, which is tasty but can be dense and dry. Best used as part of a mixture of gluten-free flours.

Gram flour – ground chickpeas, often used in Indian and Italian breads and baking.

Millet flour – a powdery yellow flour with a sweet flavour that works well in muffins and sweet breads.

Polenta/cornmeal – used in cakes and breads to help retain moisture, it also adds colour and flavour to bakes.

Potato flour – a heavy flour with a strong flavour best used sparingly. Potato starch is a different product, which does not have a strong flavour and can add moisture and a soft texture to baked goods.

Quinoa flour – rich in protein with a pleasant nutty taste, this works well in cakes, cookies and breads.

Soya flour – used mainly as a thickener, this adds a nutty flavour and a light texture to a mixture of gluten-free flours.

Tapioca flour – a starch extracted from the cassava root, native to South America. It has a sweet taste and adds texture to a mixture of gluten-free flours.

tomato focaccia

prep: 25 mins, plus rising and cooling
cook: 25-30 mins

3 tbsp olive oil,
  plus extra for brushing

200 g/7 oz buckwheat flour

200 g/7 oz potato flour

200 g/7 oz rice flour

2 tsp xanthan gum

7 g/¼ oz easy-blend dried yeast

1½ tsp salt

½ tsp black onion seeds

40 g/1½ oz sun-dried tomatoes,
  soaked, drained and chopped

600 ml/1 pint tepid water

1 small egg, beaten

2 garlic cloves, cut into slivers

few sprigs of fresh oregano

1. Brush a 33 x 23-cm/13 x 9-inch baking sheet with oil. Mix the flours, xanthan gum, yeast, salt and onion seeds in a bowl and stir in the tomatoes.

2. Make a well in the centre and stir in the water, egg and 1 tablespoon of oil to make a soft dough. Beat the dough using a wooden spoon for 4–5 minutes, then spoon into the tin, spreading evenly with a palette knife.

3. Cover with oiled clingfilm and leave in a warm place for about 1 hour, or until doubled in size. Preheat the oven to 220°C/425°F/ Gas Mark 7.

4. Press pieces of garlic and oregano into the dough at intervals. Drizzle with the remaining oil, then bake in the oven for 25–30 minutes, or until firm and golden brown. Turn out and cool on a wire rack.

top tip

Potato flour has a strong flavour and should be used in conjunction with other flours to avoid a dense bake.

cals: 2186   fat: 61g   sat fat: 9.7g   fibre: 40.6g   carbs: 373.3g   sugar: 27.3g   salt: 9.4g   protein: 56.5g

courgette & polenta bread squares

prep: 25 mins, plus cooling
cook: 30-35 mins

vegetable oil, for brushing
150 g/5½ oz polenta
100 g/3½ oz soya flour
1 tbsp gluten-free baking powder
1 tsp salt
½ tsp pepper
225 g/8 oz courgettes, grated
1 large egg, beaten
300 ml/10 fl oz unsweetened soya milk
3 tbsp olive oil

1. Preheat the oven to 190°C/375°F/Gas Mark 5. Grease a 19-cm/7½-inch square cake tin.

2. Put the polenta, flour, baking powder, salt and pepper into a bowl. Stir in the courgettes. Beat the egg, milk and oil and stir into the dry ingredients, mixing to a soft batter.

3. Spoon the mixture into the prepared tin and smooth level with a palette knife.

4. Bake in the preheated oven for 30–35 minutes, or until firm and golden brown. Leave to cool for 10 minutes in the tin, then cut into squares to serve.

top tip

Polenta, or cornmeal, can be used in baking to add colour, flavour and moisture. It is often used in muffins, but works well in this savoury bake.

cals: 169   fat: 6.7g   sat fat: 1.1g   fibre: 3.4g   carbs: 17.7g   sugar: 0.7g   salt: 1.2g   protein: 8.9g

mixed grain bread

prep: 25–30 mins, plus rising and cooling
cook: 30 mins

2½ tsp easy-blend dried yeast

450 ml/15 fl oz tepid water

1 tbsp maple syrup

120 g/4¼ oz gluten-free oat flour

175 g/6 oz rice flour, plus extra
  for dusting

175 g/6 oz almond flour

120 g/4¼ oz buckwheat flour

20 g/¾ oz tapioca flour

60 g/2¼ oz quinoa flour

1 tsp xanthan gum

1 tsp salt

3 eggs, beaten

4 tbsp sunflower oil, plus extra for oiling

1 tbsp gluten-free porridge oats

fact

There are a whole range of nut flours available in the supermarkets nowadays, including almond, chestnut, hazelnut, pecan and walnut.

1. Grease and line a 900-g/2-lb loaf tin with baking paper.

2. Mix the yeast with 125 ml/4 fl oz of the warm water and add the maple syrup. Mix well and leave at room temperature for 10–15 minutes until frothy.

3. Mix all the flours, xanthan gum and salt in a large bowl. Make a well in the middle of the mixture and add the yeast liquid.

4. Add the eggs and the sunflower oil and mix together, adding the remaining water a little at a time to form a firm dough. Turn out onto a lightly floured surface and knead for about 5 minutes until smooth and elastic.

5. Shape the loaf and place in the tin. Brush with a little water then scatter over the oats. Cover with a clean damp tea towel and leave in a warm place until the loaf has risen and is twice its size.

6. Preheat the oven to 180°C/350°F/Gas Mark 4. Bake in the preheated oven for 30 minutes, or until golden and crusty. Cool in the tin for 5 minutes then turn out onto a wire rack to cool completely.

cals: 3853   fat:197.4g   sat fat: 23.1g   fibre: 11.4g   carbs: 396.6g   sugar: 26g   salt: 6.7g   protein: 122.1g

mexican-style tortilla wraps

prep: 20-25 mins, plus cooling
cook: 40-60 mins

10 g/¼ oz easy-blend dried yeast

400 ml/14 fl oz tepid water

2 tbsp sunflower oil

400 g/14 oz gluten-free plain flour, plus extra for dusting

1½ tsp xanthan gum

2 tbsp chopped coriander (optional)

½ tsp chilli flakes (optional)

salt and pepper

1. Mix the yeast, tepid water and oil in a jug and leave at room temperature for approximately 20 minutes until frothy.

2. Sift the flour and xanthan gum into a large bowl and make a well in the centre. Add the yeast liquid to the well slowly with the coriander and chilli, if using, and season to taste. Mix to form a sticky dough. Turn out onto a floured surface and knead well. Divide into 10 small balls. Cut out a 20-cm/8-inch circle of baking paper and roll out each ball of dough under this, the thinner the better.

3. Place a frying pan over a medium heat and add the tortillas, one at a time, with the baking paper underneath. Cook for 2–3 minutes until golden. Flip over, remove the paper and cook for 2–3 minutes until golden.

4. Serve hot or cold with your favourite fillings. To store, divide each tortilla with baking paper to prevent sticking and keep in an airtight container for up to 1 week or freeze for 1–2 months.

top tip

If you bake gluten-free breads or cakes regularly, xanthan gum is a storecupboard essential. Just a small amount holds doughs together.

cals: 169   fat: 3.2g   sat fat: 0.4g   fibre: 0.9g   carbs: 32.6g   sugar: 0.2g   salt: 0.6g   protein: 2.4g

herby scones

prep: 20-25 mins, plus cooling
cook: 15-20 mins

250 g/9 oz gluten-free plain flour

60 g/2¼ oz dairy-free spread, plus extra for greasing

4 tsp gluten-free baking powder

2 tbsp finely chopped fresh herbs, such as thyme and sage

2 tbsp nutritional yeast flakes

pepper, to taste

175 ml/6 fl oz unsweetened soya milk

1 tbsp poppy seeds

1. Preheat the oven to 200°C/400°F/Gas Mark 6. Grease a large baking sheet.

2. Put the flour into a large mixing bowl. Rub in the spread using your fingertips until the texture is like soft breadcrumbs.

3. Stir in the baking powder, herbs, yeast flakes and pepper. Add the soya milk and stir the mixture with a wooden spoon to make a soft, sticky dough.

4. Turn the mixture out onto the greased baking sheet and use a palette knife or rubber spatula to shape it into a round. Use a sharp knife to mark it into eight sections and sprinkle the poppy seeds over the top.

5. Bake in the preheated oven for 15–20 minutes, or until cooked through and a skewer inserted into the loaf comes out clean. Leave to cool on the sheet for 5 minutes, then cut into sections and serve warm.

variation

You can use a mixture of fresh herbs — sage, rosemary and chives all work well.

quinoa & chive rolls

prep: 25 mins, plus rising and cooling
cook: 20–25 mins

200 g/7 oz buckwheat flour

150 g/5½ oz potato flour

2 tsp xanthan gum

1½ tsp salt

7 g/¼ oz easy-blend dried yeast

100 g/3½ oz cooked quinoa

3 tbsp snipped chives

350 ml/12 fl oz tepid water

1 small egg, beaten

1 tbsp olive oil,
  plus extra for brushing

soya milk, for glazing

1. Brush a large baking sheet with oil.

2. Sift the buckwheat flour, potato flour, xanthan gum and salt together into a bowl, then stir in the yeast, quinoa and chives.

3. Make a well in the centre and stir in the water, egg and oil to make a soft dough. Very lightly knead the dough until smooth.

4. Divide the dough into eight pieces and shape each piece into a smooth ball. Arrange on the prepared baking sheet, cover and leave in a warm place for about 1 hour, or until doubled in size. Meanwhile, preheat the oven to 200°C/400°F/Gas Mark 6.

5. Brush the rolls with soya milk to glaze. Bake in the preheated oven for 20–25 minutes, or until firm and golden brown. Transfer to a wire rack to cool.

fact

Quinoa is rich in protein and has a pleasantly nutty taste that works well in bakes and breads.

2

makes 8

cals: 200   fat: 4.2g   sat fat: 0.7g   fibre: 4.3g   carbs: 36.4g   sugar: 1.3g   salt: 1.2g   protein: 6.1g

fruit soda bread

prep: 25 mins, plus standing
cook: 25-30 mins

55 g/2 oz ready-to-eat stoned prunes, chopped

55 g/2 oz ready-to-eat dried apricots, chopped

40 g/1½ oz ready-to-eat dried apples, chopped

40 g/1½ oz dried cranberries

150 ml/5 fl oz pure apple juice

450 g/1 lb gluten-free plain flour

1½ tbsp gluten-free baking powder

2 tsp xanthan gum

¼ tsp salt

2 tbsp sunflower oil, plus extra for greasing

225 ml/8 fl oz unsweetened soya milk, plus extra for brushing

4 tbsp maple syrup

1 tbsp pumpkin seeds

dairy-free spread, to serve (optional)

1. Place the prunes, apricots, apples and cranberries in a bowl and pour over the apple juice. Cover and leave to stand for about 30 minutes.

2. Preheat the oven to 200°C/400°F/Gas Mark 6. Brush a baking tray with oil. Sift the flour, baking powder, xanthan gum and salt into a bowl and make a well in the centre.

3. Mix the oil, milk and maple syrup and add to the dry ingredients with the fruits and juice, mixing lightly to a soft, but not sticky, dough. Add a little more milk if the dough feels dry.

4. Shape the dough to a smooth round on the prepared baking tray, flatten slightly and cut a deep cross through the centre almost to the base. Gently pull the wedges apart at the points. Brush with milk and sprinkle with pumpkin seeds.

5. Bake in the preheated oven for 25–30 minutes, or until golden brown and the base sounds hollow when tapped. Serve in chunks with dairy-free spread, if desired.

cals: 2788   fat: 48.7g   sat fat: 6.2g   fibre: 25.6g   carbs: 557.4g   sugar: 164.1g   salt: 8g   protein: 36.4g

Baking without gluten or dairy presents some challenges. Gluten-free cakes might not rise as well and many recipes rely on butter to provide the fat, but this isn't an option for dairy-free cakes! This chapter contains tried-and-tested recipes developed using techniques and ingredients to ensure successful bakes.

baking & desserts

angel food cake —————————————→ 156

raspberry & chocolate cake ———→ 158

carrot & walnut cake ——————————→ 160

cookies & cream cupcakes ————→ 162

almond cupcakes ————————————→ 164

blueberry & oatmeal muffins ——→ 166

peach & vanilla muffins ——————→ 168

lemon meringue cookies ————→ 170

HIDDEN GLUTEN ————————————→ 172

mocha cookies ———————————→ 174

coconut squares ————————→ 176

raw chocolate ice cream ————→ 178

creamy coconut & mango quinoa —→ 180

apple & cinnamon pie ——————→ 182

rhubarb & blackberry crumble —→ 184

fig & watermelon salad —————→ 186

baked plums with port ————→ 188

chilli chocolate sponge puddings —→ 190

angel food cake

prep: 25-30 mins, plus standing and cooling
cook: 50-55 mins

oil, for greasing
10 egg whites
60 g/2¼ oz white rice flour
60 g/2¼ oz tapioca flour
60 g/2¼ oz gluten-free cornflour
60 g/2¼ oz potato flour
300 g/10½ oz caster sugar
1½ tsp gluten-free cream of tartar
½ tsp vanilla extract
½ tsp salt
500 g/1 lb 2 oz bag of frozen fruits of
   the forest (optional)
85 g/3 oz caster sugar (optional)
gluten-free icing sugar, to decorate

top tip

This is a very light and delicate cake, so make sure that the cake is left to cool upside-down in the tin on a wire rack to help keep its shape.

1. Preheat the oven to 180°C/350°F/Gas Mark 4. Grease a 20-cm/8-inch cake tin and line with baking paper.

2. Allow the egg whites to sit for about 30 minutes at room temperature in a large bowl. In a separate bowl, sift the white rice flour, tapioca flour, cornflour, potato flour and 175 g/6 oz of the sugar.

3. Using an electric mixer, beat the egg whites with the cream of tartar, vanilla extract and salt until soft peaks form.

4. Gradually add the remaining 125 g/4½ oz of sugar, beating until stiff peaks develop. Add the flour mixture and fold in.

5. Spoon the mixture into the prepared tin and bake in the preheated oven for approximately 45 minutes, or until firm to the touch and a skewer inserted in the centre comes out clean.

6. Remove from the oven and, leaving the cake in the tin, turn upside-down to cool on a wire rack. Poach the fruits of the forest with the caster sugar gently until soft. Allow to cool completely. When the cake is cool, remove from the tin and decorate with icing sugar and the drained mixed fruit, if desired.

cals: 187   fat: 0.2g   sat fat: trace   fibre: 0.5g   carbs: 43.1g   sugar: 26.2g   salt: 0.4g   protein: 3.7g

raspberry & chocolate cake

prep: 30 mins, plus cooling
cook: 50-55 mins

dairy-free spread or oil,
  for greasing

300 g/10½ oz gluten-free plain flour

50 g/1¾ oz gluten and dairy-free
  cocoa powder

½ tsp xanthan gum

1 tsp gluten-free baking powder

1 tsp gluten-free bicarbonate of soda

½ tsp salt

300 g/10½ oz granulated sugar

375 ml/13 fl oz soya milk

125 ml/4 fl oz rapeseed oil

7 tbsp gluten-free seedless
  raspberry jam

1 tsp vanilla extract

icing

45 ml/1½ fl oz soya milk

85 g/3 oz gluten and dairy-free
  plain chocolate, broken into
  small pieces

60 g/2¼ oz gluten-free icing sugar

1 tbsp maple syrup

fresh raspberries, to decorate

1. Preheat the oven to 180°C/350°F/Gas Mark 4. Grease a 23-cm/9-inch round cake tin and line with baking paper.

2. Sift the flour, cocoa, xanthan gum, baking powder and bicarbonate of soda into a large bowl and stir in the salt and sugar. Pour the soya milk into a saucepan and add the oil, raspberry jam and vanilla extract. Place over a medium heat and whisk to combine. Stir into the dry ingredients and mix thoroughly.

3. Transfer to the prepared cake tin and bake in the preheated oven for 45 minutes, or until a skewer inserted into the centre comes out clean. Turn out and leave to cool completely on a wire rack before icing.

4. To make the icing, heat the soya milk in a small saucepan over a medium heat until it reaches boiling point, then drop the chocolate into the pan and stir until completely melted. Remove from the heat and whisk in the icing sugar and maple syrup. Set aside to cool before icing the cake, using a palette knife. Top with a few fresh raspberries before slicing and serving.

cals: 389   fat: 14.6g   sat fat: 2.8g   fibre: 3.2g   carbs: 63.8g   sugar: 38.1g   salt: 0.6g   protein: 3.8g

carrot & walnut cake

prep: 25-30 mins, plus cooling and setting
cook: 1 hour

dairy-free spread, for greasing

225 g/8 oz gluten-free self-raising flour

2 tsp gluten-free baking powder

115 g/4 oz brown sugar

2 tsp ground cinnamon

1 tsp ground nutmeg

85 g/3 oz walnuts, roughly chopped

225 g/8 oz carrots, grated

125 ml/4 fl oz maple syrup

125 ml/4 fl oz rapeseed oil

cream cheese frosting

115 g/4 oz gluten and dairy-free cream cheese

55 g/2 oz dairy-free spread

225 g/8 oz gluten-free icing sugar

1. Preheat the oven to 160°C/325°F/Gas Mark 3. Grease an 18-cm/7-inch round, loose-based cake tin and line with baking paper.

2. Sift the flour and baking powder into a large mixing bowl. Stir in the sugar, cinnamon, nutmeg and walnuts and mix well with a wooden spoon.

3. Stir the carrots into the dry ingredients, along with the maple syrup and rapeseed oil, and mix well with a wooden spoon.

4. Spoon the mixture into the prepared cake tin, smooth with a rubber spatula and bake in the preheated oven for 1 hour, or until a skewer inserted into the centre of the cake comes out clean. Leave in the tin to firm up for 10 minutes, then transfer to a wire rack and allow to cool completely before frosting.

5. To make the frosting, beat the cream cheese, spread and icing sugar together until smooth. Using an electric food mixer or a hand-held electric mixer is easiest for this, but you can do it with a fork if necessary. Spread the filling generously on the top of the cake, and on the sides too if you like, and swirl the surface into an attractive pattern with a fork. Leave to set before serving.

cals: 394   fat: 19.8g   sat fat: 2.6g   fibre: 1.5g   carbs: 53.8g   sugar: 35.8g   salt: 0.5g   protein: 2.6g

cookies & cream cupcakes

prep: 30-35 mins, plus standing and cooling
cook: 18-20 mins

250 ml/9 fl oz soya milk

1 tsp gluten-free cider vinegar

150 g/5½ oz caster sugar

75 ml/2½ fl oz rapeseed oil

1 tsp vanilla extract

150 g/5½ oz gluten-free plain flour

25 g/1 oz gluten and dairy-free
  cocoa powder

¾ tsp gluten-free bicarbonate
  of soda

½ tsp gluten-free baking powder

70 g/2½ oz gluten and dairy-free
  cookies, crumbled

topping

35 g/1¼ oz dairy-free spread

35 g/1¼ oz white vegetable
  shortening

300 g/10½ oz gluten-free
  icing sugar

¾ tsp vanilla extract

75 ml/2½ fl oz soya cream

35 g/1¼ oz gluten and dairy-free
  cookies, crumbled

1. Preheat the oven to 180°C/350°F/Gas Mark 4. Line a 12-hole cupcake tin with paper cases.

2. Put the soya milk into a measuring jug, stir in the vinegar and set aside for a few minutes to curdle.

3. Put the sugar, oil and vanilla into a large mixing bowl and beat together. Pour in the milk and vinegar, mix thoroughly and then add the flour, cocoa powder, bicarbonate of soda and baking powder. Stir until the ingredients are just combined, then fold in the cookie crumbs.

4. Divide the mixture evenly between the paper cases and bake in the preheated oven for 18–20 minutes, or until springy to the touch and golden. Transfer to a wire rack to cool completely before icing.

5. To make the topping, beat the spread and vegetable shortening together, then mix in the icing sugar and the vanilla. Gradually add the soya cream to achieve a thick pipeable consistency. Pipe or spoon the icing generously over the cupcakes and sprinkle with cookie crumbs.

cals: 342   fat: 13.7g   sat fat: 3.1g   fibre: 1.1g   carbs: 55g   sugar: 37.8g   salt: 0.3g   protein: 2.1g

almond cupcakes

prep: 25-30 mins, plus cooling
cook: 25-30 mins

5 tbsp rapeseed oil
4 tbsp plain soya yogurt
160 ml/5½ fl oz soya milk
160 g/5¾ oz caster sugar
3 tbsp almond extract
40 g/1½ oz ground almonds
160 g/5¾ oz gluten-free plain flour
½ tsp xanthan gum
1½ tsp gluten-free baking powder
½ tsp salt

icing

60 g/2¼ oz gluten and dairy-free white
  chocolate, broken into pieces
100 g/3½ oz gluten-free icing sugar
1½ tbsp soya milk
toasted flaked almonds,
  to decorate

1. Preheat the oven to 180°C/350°F/Gas Mark 4. Line a cupcake tin with 10 paper cases.

2. Place the oil, yogurt, milk, sugar, almond extract and ground almonds in a large bowl. Sift in the flour, xanthan gum, baking powder and salt then beat until combined.

3. Divide the mixture between the cases in the prepared tin and bake in the preheated oven for 20–25 minutes, or until well risen and golden. Transfer the cupcakes to a wire rack and leave to cool completely before icing.

4. Melt the chocolate in a heatproof bowl set over a pan of simmering water. Remove from the heat and leave to cool. Beat in the icing sugar and milk. Spread over the cupcakes with a spoon. Top with a few toasted almonds.

top tip

If you would like these cupcakes to look more special, replace the flaked almonds with gold balls.

blueberry & oatmeal muffins

prep: 20–25 mins, plus cooling
cook: 20–25 mins

250 ml/9 fl oz pure orange juice

60 g/2¼ oz gluten-free porridge oats

100 g/3½ oz caster sugar

200 g/7 oz gluten-free plain flour, sifted

½ tsp xanthan gum

1½ tsp gluten-free baking powder

½ tsp gluten-free bicarbonate of soda

½ tsp cinnamon

¼ tsp mixed spice

125 ml/4 fl oz vegetable oil

1 egg, beaten

1 tsp glycerine

175 g/6 oz blueberries

demerara sugar, to sprinkle

1. Preheat the oven to 180°C/350°F/Gas Mark 4. Line a 9-hole muffin tin with paper cases.

2. Add the orange juice to the porridge oats and mix well in a bowl. In a separate bowl, mix the sugar, flour, xanthan gum, baking powder, bicarbonate of soda and spices. Add the oil, egg and glycerine to the dry mixture and mix well. Then add the oat mixture and blueberries and fold these in gently.

3. Divide the mixture between the muffin cases and sprinkle with the sugar. Bake in the preheated oven for 20–25 minutes, or until a skewer comes out clean when inserted. Leave to cool on a wire rack.

variation

To create another classic muffin flavour, replace the blueberries with the same amount of fresh cranberries.

cals: 319   fat: 15.2g   sat fat: 1.3g   fibre: 1.6g   carbs: 43.7g   sugar: 19.7g   salt: 0.4g   protein: 3.3g

peach & vanilla muffins

prep: 30-35 mins, plus cooling and standing
cook: 35-40 mins

3–4 ripe peaches (approx. 450 g/1 lb),
  stoned, cut into eighths

juice of ½ lemon

3 tbsp maple syrup

350 g/12 oz gluten-free plain flour

1 tsp gluten-free baking powder

½ tsp gluten-free bicarbonate of soda

1 tsp linseed meal

100 g/3½ oz brown sugar

125 ml/4 fl oz soya milk

1 tbsp gluten-free white
  wine vinegar

1 tbsp vanilla extract

90 ml/3 fl oz rapeseed oil

70 g/2½ oz gluten-free
  peach preserve

1. Preheat the oven to 180°C/350°F/Gas Mark 4. Line a 12-hole muffin tin with paper cases.

2. Place the peaches in a shallow baking dish. Pour the lemon juice and maple syrup over the peaches and bake in the preheated oven for 15 minutes. Set aside to cool completely. Leave the oven on.

3. Sift the flour, baking powder and bicarbonate of soda into a large mixing bowl. Stir in the linseed meal and sugar. Put the soya milk into a jug, stir in the vinegar and set aside for a few minutes to curdle.

4. Put half of the peaches and the juice from the baking tin into a food processor. Add the vanilla extract and rapeseed oil and pulse to a purée. Roughly chop the remaining peaches. Stir the milk mixture and peach purée into the dry ingredients, using a rubber spatula, until just combined. Fold in the chopped peaches.

5. Divide the mixture equally between the paper cases and bake in the preheated oven for 20–25 minutes, or until risen and springy to the touch. Transfer to a wire rack to cool.

6. To make the peach glaze, put the preserve into a small saucepan with 1 tablespoon of water. Bring to the boil, stirring continuously with a wooden spatula as the mixture boils vigorously for 1 minute. Remove the pan from the heat and continue to stir for a further 30 seconds. Brush the warm glaze over the muffins and allow to cool before serving.

lemon meringue cookies

prep: 20–25 mins, plus cooling
cook: 1½ hours

2 large egg whites
⅛ tsp gluten-free cream of tartar
pinch of salt
140 g/5 oz caster sugar
finely grated zest of 1 lemon

1. Preheat the oven to 110°C/225°F/Gas Mark ¼. Line a large baking sheet with baking paper.

2. In a large, greasefree bowl, beat the egg whites with an electric mixer until they are frothy. Add the cream of tartar and salt and continue to beat on high until soft peaks form. Gradually add the sugar and continue to beat on high for about 3–4 minutes or until stiff peaks form. Fold in the lemon zest.

3. Drop the mixture in rounded teaspoons onto the prepared baking sheet. Bake in the preheated oven for about 1½ hours, or until dry and crisp but not yet beginning to colour. Turn off the oven and leave the cookies inside the oven for a further 30 minutes. Serve at room temperature.

top tip

Meringues store well in an airtight container so make them in advance for unexpected guests!

cals: 73   fat: trace   sat fat: trace   fibre: 0.1g   carbs: 17.7g   sugar: 17.6g   salt: 0.3g   protein: 0.7g

hidden gluten

Hidden gluten can be found in the most unsuspecting of foods. As gluten is most commonly found in flour, removing products such as bread, cake and biscuits from a diet is perceived as a gluten-free diet; however this is not the case. Gluten is used in many processed products and is hidden in everyday foods.

stay safe

Cross contamination

Cross contamination can occur very easily in the kitchen. Toasters, grills, pans, chopping boards, utensils, appliances and oils that were used for preparing or cooking foods containing gluten may still have traces of gluten in them which can contaminate your gluten-free food. It is essential that a strict cleaning regime is adhered to in order to eliminate the risk of cross-contamination. Cooking oil which has been used to deep-fry foods containing gluten or coated with a gluten containing product such as breadcrumbs, should never be reused to fry gluten-free food. Care should also be taken when baking with ordinary flour as residues of flour can remain in the air for up to 24 hours and settle on counters and gluten-free food such as fresh fruit. It is also important to be vigilant for crumbs in foods like butter which can be passed from knives used for spreading on non gluten-free bread. Gluten-free foods should be stored separately in the kitchen, separate chopping boards should be used and a separate toaster should be used to make gluten-free toast. Gluten can also be found in medicines, vitamins and supplements, lipstick, make-up, toothpaste, body lotions and creams so it is important to bear this in mind when using these products and to ask for gluten-free alternatives.

Hidden gluten when eating out

Some restaurants today offer gluten-free items on their menus and, if not, many good

chefs are now willing to provide a gluten-free alternative on request. However, this is not always the case and catering professionals need to be better informed with regards to gluten-free products. Hidden gluten is in many prepared and processed foods. Therefore, when eating out it is essential that you do not eat anything that is cooked with sauces, dressings or creams unless it is stated as being gluten-free on the menu. The best way to reduce the risk is to keep your food as plain as possible. It is also better to ask for the meat or fish to be cooked in olive oil to prevent contamination.

Hidden gluten in foods

The following foods may contain gluten, but there are gluten-free alternatives to many:

- ketchup and some sauces
- dry-roasted nuts
- sweets and confectionery
- crisps
- canned baked beans
- canned or packet soups
- commercial salad dressings
- mustard
- some marinades
- soy sauce
- frozen chips
- pretzels
- Bombay mix
- scotch eggs
- white pepper
- powdered gravy and sauce mixes
- frozen meals
- hamburgers and sausages
- processed meat
- hot dogs
- drinking chocolate and malted milk drinks
- beer, lager, stout or ale
- some fizzy drinks

mocha cookies

prep: 20-25 mins, plus cooling
cook: 15 mins

115 g/4 oz gluten-free plain flour

¼ tsp gluten-free baking powder

15 g/½ oz gluten and dairy-free cocoa powder

125 g/4½ oz brown sugar

1 tbsp gluten-free espresso powder

125 g/4½ oz dairy-free spread

50 g/1¾ oz gluten-free porridge oats

1. Preheat the oven to 180°C/350°F/Gas Mark 4. Line a large baking sheet with baking paper.

2. Sift together the flour, baking powder and cocoa powder in a large mixing bowl. Add the sugar and combine thoroughly.

3. Dissolve the espresso powder in 1 tablespoon of boiling water and stir into the bowl. Add the spread and oats and mix thoroughly to form a soft dough.

4. Form the mixture into 14 small balls, place on the prepared baking sheet and flatten slightly. Leave spaces between the cookies as they will expand during cooking. Bake in the preheated oven for 15 minutes, or until crisp.

5. Transfer to a wire rack to cool, using a palette knife. Leave to cool completely before serving or storing in an airtight jar for up to five days.

top tip

These are easy to make for bake sales or coffee mornings where there's a need to cater for all diets.

cals: 136   fat: 6.5g   sat fat: 1.5g   fibre: 1.5g   carbs: 18.5g   sugar: 9g   salt: 0.1g   protein: 1.4g

coconut squares

prep: 25 mins, plus chilling
cook: 25-30 mins

225 ml/8 fl oz coconut cream
250 g/9 oz caster sugar
300 g/10½ oz desiccated coconut
1 tsp ground cardamom
¼ tsp beetroot powder

1. Line an 18-cm/7-inch square baking tin with clingfilm.

2. Put the coconut cream into a saucepan with the sugar. Heat gently until melted. Bring to boiling point and then simmer, stirring continuously, for 20 minutes until reduced to a thick syrup. If you have a sugar thermometer, check that the temperature is around 104°C/220°F. If you don't have a sugar thermometer, drop a little of the syrup onto a cold plate, wait for a minute and then carefully test it with your finger. It's ready when the surface wrinkles when you push the edge.

3. Stir in the coconut and cardamom, mix thoroughly with a wooden spoon and then spoon half of the mixture into the lined baking tin. Press down firmly to form a smooth layer in the bottom of the tin. Mix the beetroot powder with 2 teaspoons of water and then mix it into the remaining coconut mixture. Make sure it is well distributed. Spoon the pink coconut into the tin and press it into a firm layer over the white coconut.

4. Put the coconut mixture into a refrigerator to chill for at least 4 hours, or overnight. Then turn it out of the tin and use a sharp knife to cut it into 20 squares.

makes 20

fact

These coconut squares are a gluten- and dairy-free take on the classic coconut ice.

cals: 226   fat: 17.2g   sat fat: 14.7g   fibre: 2.6g   carbs: 18.7g   sugar: 13.6g   salt: trace   protein: 1.9g

raw chocolate ice cream

prep: 15 mins, plus freezing
cook: no cooking

3 bananas (approx. 300 g/10½ oz)
3 tbsp raw cocoa powder
1 tbsp agave nectar

1. Peel the bananas and cut them into
2-cm/¾-inch pieces. Place in a freezer bag
and freeze for 3 hours.

2. Take the bananas from the freezer and
place in a food processor or blender with
the cocoa powder and agave nectar. Process
until smooth.

3. Serve immediately or refreeze if you prefer
a firmer consistency.

top tip

This is a healthier dairy-free version of
traditional ice cream which is loaded with
high-fat cream. In this good-for-you recipe,
the cream is replaced with healthy bananas.

cals: 112   fat: 0.7g   sat fat: 0.4g   fibre: 3.7g   carbs: 26.9g   sugar: 14.6g   salt: trace   protein: 1.9g

creamy coconut & mango quinoa

prep: 20 mins, plus cooling and standing
cook: 20–25 mins, plus standing

300 ml/10 fl oz canned coconut milk

115 g/4 oz white quinoa, rinsed

1 large ripe mango, about 550 g/1 lb 4 oz

75 g/2¾ oz caster sugar

juice of 1 large lime

4-cm/1½-inch piece fresh ginger, sliced into chunks

100 g/3½ oz blueberries

4 tbsp toasted coconut chips

4 lime wedges, to decorate

1. Put the coconut milk and quinoa into a small saucepan and bring to the boil. Cover and simmer for 15–20 minutes, or until most of the liquid has evaporated. Remove from the heat, but leave covered for a further 10 minutes to allow the grains to swell. Fluff up with a fork, tip into a bowl and leave to cool.

2. Meanwhile, peel the mango, discard the stone and roughly chop the flesh (you will need 350 g/12 oz). Put the mango into a food processor with the sugar and lime juice. Squeeze the ginger in a garlic press and add the juice to the mango mixture. Process for 30 seconds to make a smooth purée.

3. Mix the mango mixture into the cooled quinoa and leave to stand for 30 minutes.

4. Divide the mixture between four bowls and sprinkle with the blueberries and coconut chips. Decorate with lime wedges and serve.

fact

Sweet, juicy mangoes contain more vitamins and carotenes than most other fruits. They are also high in fibre and low on the glycaemic index.

cals: 438   fat: 21.5g   sat fat: 17.4g   fibre: 5.2g   carbs: 60.1g   sugar: 34g   salt: trace   protein: 6.9g

apple & cinnamon pie

prep: 30 mins, plus cooling
cook: 35–40 mins

pastry

60 g/2¼ oz white vegetable shortening

15 g/½ oz dairy-free spread

225 g/8 oz gluten-free plain flour, plus extra for dusting

1 tbsp gluten-free baking powder

pinch of salt

soya milk, for brushing

caster sugar, for sprinkling

filling

1 kg/2 lb 4 oz cooking apples, peeled, cored and sliced

150 g/5½ oz caster sugar

2 tsp gluten-free cornflour

1 tbsp ground cinnamon

1. To make the pastry, place the shortening and spread in a bowl. Pour in 100 ml/3½ fl oz of boiling water and mix with a wooden spoon until creamy. Add the flour, baking powder and salt, stir together, then turn out onto a lightly floured work surface and knead into a smooth ball. Leave to cool for 5 minutes. Roll out on a sheet of clingfilm to a shape that slightly overhangs a 23-cm/9-inch round pie dish. Set aside.

2. Preheat the oven to 180°C/350°F/Gas Mark 4.

3. Place the apples in a large saucepan with the sugar, cornflour and cinnamon, and add 3 tablespoons of water. Cook gently for 5–10 minutes, or until the apple is just tender and most of the liquid in the pan has been thickened by the cornflour. Leave to cool.

4. Put the apple filling into the pie dish. Lift the pastry on the sheet of clingfilm (to support it) and transfer the pastry to the top of the pie, pressing the edges down and trimming away any excess with a sharp knife. Re-roll the trimmings to make decorative leaves and place these on top of the pie.

5. Brush the top of the pie with a little soya milk and sprinkle with a little caster sugar. Bake in the preheated oven for 30 minutes, or until just golden. Serve hot or cold.

cals: 308   fat: 8.7g   sat fat: 3.6g   fibre: 2.3g   carbs: 58.7g   sugar: 31.5g   salt: 0.6g   protein: 1.8g

rhubarb & blackberry crumble

prep: 20-25 mins
cook: 47-55 mins

8–10 sticks of rhubarb, cut into bite-sized pieces (800 g/1 lb 12 oz total weight)

8 tbsp caster sugar

250 g/9 oz blackberries

½ tsp vanilla extract

½ tsp ground ginger

crumble topping

100 g/3½ oz dairy-free spread, plus extra for greasing

200 g/7 oz gluten-free plain flour

100 g/3½ oz demerara sugar

15 g/½ oz flaked almonds

1. Preheat the oven to 180°C/350°F/Gas Mark 4.

2. Place the rhubarb on a baking tray, sprinkle with the caster sugar and roast in the oven for 12–15 minutes.

3. Place the baked rhubarb in a 23-cm/9-inch greased ovenproof dish with the blackberries, vanilla extract and ginger. Stir well to combine.

4. For the topping, rub the spread and flour together with your fingertips until it resembles fine breadcrumbs. Add the sugar and almonds and mix together. Cover the rhubarb mixture with the crumble topping and bake in the preheated oven for 35–40 minutes until golden. Serve immediately.

serves 6

variation

If you can't get hold of blackberries then either raspberries or chopped strawberries would work as well.

cals: 430 fat: 14.3g sat fat: 3g fibre: 5.3g carbs: 74.1g sugar: 40.4g salt: 0.1g protein: 4g

fig & watermelon salad

prep: 25-30 mins, plus cooling and chilling
cook: 5 mins

1 watermelon, weighing about
   1.5 kg/3 lb 5 oz
115 g/4 oz seedless black grapes
4 figs

syrup dressing
1 lime
grated rind and juice of 1 orange
1 tbsp maple syrup
2 tbsp clear honey

1. Cut the watermelon into quarters and scoop out and discard the seeds. Cut the flesh away from the rind, then chop the flesh into 2.5-cm/1-inch cubes. Place the watermelon cubes in a bowl with the grapes. Cut each fig lengthways into eight wedges and add to the bowl.

2. Grate the lime and mix the rind with the orange rind and juice, maple syrup and honey in a small saucepan. Bring to the boil over a low heat. Pour the mixture over the fruit and stir. Leave to cool. Stir the fruit again, cover and chill in the refrigerator for at least 1 hour, stirring occasionally.

3. Divide the fruit salad equally between four bowls and serve.

variation

Instead of grapes, try adding the same weight of fresh blackberries or blueberries for a different flavour.

baked plums with port

prep: 20 mins, plus cooling
cook: 40-55 mins

8 large plums
1 cinnamon stick
2 strips pared orange rind
25 g/1 oz soft light brown sugar
2 tbsp light agave nectar
200 ml/7 fl oz port

1. Preheat the oven to 180°C/350°F/Gas Mark 4. Halve and stone the plums.

2. Place the plum halves cut-side up in a small baking dish with the cinnamon stick and orange rind. Sprinkle over the sugar. Mix together the agave and port and pour around the plums.

3. Bake in the preheated oven for 30–40 minutes, or until the plums are soft. Leave to cool for 5 minutes, then pour off the liquid into a small saucepan.

4. Bring the liquid to the boil, then simmer for 5–10 minutes, or until syrupy and reduced by about one third. Pour the syrup over the plums. Serve immediately.

fact

Plums are full of antioxidants that protect the brain as well as the heart

cals: 178   fat: 0.4g   sat fat: trace   fibre: 2.1g   carbs: 31.3g   sugar: 29.1g   salt: trace   protein: 1g

chilli chocolate sponge puddings

prep: 20-25 mins, plus cooling
cook: 45 mins

70 g/2½ oz dairy-free spread, plus extra for greasing

50 ml/2 fl oz maple syrup

55 g/2 oz gluten-free plain flour

3 tbsp gluten and dairy-free cocoa powder

½ tsp gluten-free baking powder

70 g/2½ oz ground almonds

pinch of gluten-free chilli powder

sauce

225 g/8 oz gluten and dairy-free plain chocolate, broken into pieces

85 g/3 oz caster sugar

125 ml/4 fl oz soya cream

pinch of gluten-free chilli powder

1. Preheat the oven to 150°C/300°F/Gas Mark 2. Grease and line four ramekins.

2. Cream the spread and maple syrup together with a wooden spoon. Add the flour, cocoa powder, baking powder, ground almonds and chilli powder and mix thoroughly. Divide the mixture evenly between the ramekins.

3. Place the ramekins on a baking tray and bake in the preheated oven for 40 minutes, or until springy to the touch. Leave to cool slightly and then turn out onto serving plates.

4. To make the sauce, place the chocolate in a small saucepan with the sugar, soya cream and 50 ml/2 fl oz boiling water. Heat gently to melt the chocolate and stir together thoroughly. Add the chilli powder, according to your taste. Pour the sauce over the puddings then serve immediately.

variation

More subtle spices, such as cinnamon and ground ginger, also work well in this recipe.

cals: 765   fat: 48.8g   sat fat: 17.8g   fibre: 9.4g   carbs: 74g   sugar: 43.2g   salt: 0.4g   protein: 10.5g

index

angel food cake 156
apples
    apple & cinnamon pie 182
    apple & seed muesli 18
    fruit compote with quinoa 20
    fruit soda bread 152
    raw shoots & seeds super salad 93
    shaker salad in a jar 68
apricots
    apricot & raisin oat bars 22
    fruit compote with quinoa 20
    fruit soda bread 152
    millet porridge with apricot
        topping 14
    raw shoots & seeds super salad 93
avocados
    easy vegetable sushi 72
    monkfish ceviche with red quinoa 74

bananas
    banana & brazil nut loaf 42
    berry sunrise smoothie 10
    fruit, nut & seed trail mix 48
    raw chocolate ice cream 178
beans
    chicken chilli 96
    jamaican rice & peas with tofu 104
    salsa bean dip 52
beef
    beef fried rice 90
    chimichurri steak 102
    seared beef salad 66
beetroot hash, red 34
berries
    berry sunrise smoothie 10
    blueberry & oatmeal muffins 166
    creamy coconut & mango
        quinoa 180
    date & seed power balls 46
    fruit compote with quinoa 20
    fruit soda bread 152
    honey & blueberry bars 24
    raspberry & chocolate cake 158
    raw buckwheat & almond porridge 16
    rhubarb & blackberry crumble 184
    seared beef salad 66
    strawberry & vanilla soya shake 12
buckwheat
    apple & seed muesli 18
    raw buckwheat & almond porridge 16

carrot & walnut cake 160
chicken
    chicken balls with dipping sauce 76
    chicken chilli 96
    jambalaya 114
    mexican chicken with rice 84
    roast chicken 116
    spatchcocked chicken with lemon 106
    warm chicken & mango salad 62
chickpea bread, italian 134
chocolate 65
    chilli chocolate sponge puddings 190

date & seed power balls 46
mocha cookies 174
raspberry & chocolate cake 158
raw chocolate ice cream 178
coconut 65
    breakfast cookies 28
    coconut squares 176
    crab & ginger soup 60
    creamy coconut & mango quinoa 180
    date & seed power balls 46
    fruit compote with quinoa 20
    grilled salmon with mango & lime
        salsa 98
    jamaican rice & peas with tofu 104
    thai fish curry 112
cookies & cream cupcakes 162
coriander flatbreads 136
courgettes
    courgette & polenta bread
        squares 142
    courgette loaf 40
    hot & sour courgettes 128
    roasted vegetables 124
cracker bites 54

dates
    apple & seed muesli 18
    date & seed power balls 46
    fruit, nut & seed trail mix 48

edamame beans
    ginger & miso stir-fry 110
    vietnamese tofu & noodle salad 78
eggs
    beef fried rice 90
    eggs in pepper & tomato sauce 38
    potato & onion frittata 32
    red beetroot hash 34
    sausage & potato omelette 36

fig & watermelon salad 186
fish & seafood
    crab & ginger soup 60
    five-spice tuna steaks 82
    grilled salmon with mango & lime
        salsa 98
    jambalaya 114
    monkfish ceviche with red quinoa 74
    thai fish curry 112

grapes
    fig & watermelon salad 186
    kiwi quencher juice 8

ham: green lentil & vegetable soup 58

kiwi quencher juice 8

lemon meringue cookies 170
lentils
    green lentil & vegetable soup 58
    sweet potato & lentil stew 88

mangoes
    creamy coconut & mango
        quinoa 180
    grilled salmon with mango & lime
        salsa 98
    warm chicken & mango salad 62
millet
    apple & seed muesli 18
    millet porridge with apricot
        topping 14

noodles
    spring rolls 126
    vietnamese tofu & noodle salad 78
nuts
    almond cupcakes 164
    banana & brazil nut loaf 42
    breakfast cookies 28
    carrot & walnut cake 160
    courgette loaf 40
    date & seed power balls 46
    fruit, nut & seed trail mix 48
    ginger & miso stir-fry 110
    honey & blueberry bars 24
    nutty toffee popcorn 56
    raw buckwheat & almond porridge 16
    raw shoots & seeds super salad 93
    warm chicken & mango salad 62

oats
    apricot & raisin oat bars 22
    blueberry & oatmeal muffins 166
    fruit, nut & seed trail mix 48
    mixed grain bread 144
    mocha cookies 174

pak choi
    five-spice tuna steaks 82
    pork meatballs in a chilli broth 108
    spicy pak choi with sesame
        sauce 122
peach & vanilla muffins 168
peppers
    crab & ginger soup 60
    creole turkey-stuffed peppers 86
    easy vegetable sushi 72
    eggs in pepper & tomato sauce 38
    ginger & miso stir-fry 110
    roasted vegetables 124
plums, baked with port 188
pork
    barbecue-glazed spare ribs 92
    pork meatballs in a chilli broth 108
    spring rolls 126
potatoes
    potato & onion frittata 32
    sausage & potato omelette 36
prunes
    fruit compote with quinoa 20
    fruit soda bread 152

quinoa
    creamy coconut & mango
        quinoa 180

fruit compote with quinoa 20
honey & blueberry bars 24
monkfish ceviche with red quinoa 74
potato & onion frittata 32
quinoa & chive rolls 150

rhubarb & blackberry crumble 184
rice
    beef fried rice 90
    creole turkey-stuffed peppers 86
    easy vegetable sushi 72
    jamaican rice & peas with tofu 104
    jambalaya 114
    spiced basmati rice 130

sausages
    jambalaya 114
    sausage & potato omelette 36
scones, herby 148
seeds
    apple & seed muesli 18
    date & seed power balls 46
    fruit, nut & seed trail mix 48
    fruit soda bread 152
    raw shoots & seeds super salad 93
    seven grain bread 132
    spicy pak choi with sesame sauce 122
sprouting seeds & beans
    raw shoots & seeds super salad 93
    shaker salad in a jar 68
sweet potatoes
    red beetroot hash 34
    sweet potato & lentil stew 88
    sweet potato chips 50
sweetcorn
    chimichurri steak 102
    crab & ginger soup 60

tofu
    berry sunrise smoothie 10
    herby tofu scramble 30
    jamaican rice & peas with tofu 104
    vietnamese tofu & noodle salad 78
tomatoes
    eggs in pepper & tomato sauce 38
    herby tofu scramble 30
    mexican chicken with rice 84
    polenta bruschettas with tapenade 70
    salsa bean dip 52
    sausage & potato omelette 36
    tomato focaccia 140
tortilla wraps, mexican-style 146
turkey-stuffed peppers, creole 86

vegetable pakoras 120